PIANO • VOCAL • GUITAR

W9-BWQ-020

THE BEST SONGS EVER

*These songs are the property of:

The Bourne Co.
Music Publishers
5 West 37th Street
New York, NY 10018

ISBN 0-7935-0445-7

HAL•LEONARD® CORPORATION
7777 W. BLUEMOUND RD. P.O. BOX 13819 MILWAUKEE, WI 53213

For all works contained herein:
Unauthorized copying, arranging, adapting, recording or public performance is an infringement of copyright.
Infringers are liable under the law.

Visit Hal Leonard Online at
www.halleonard.com

ALL I ASK OF YOU
from THE PHANTOM OF THE OPERA

Music by ANDREW LLOYD WEBBER
Lyrics by CHARLES HART
Additional Lyrics by RICHARD STILGOE

Andante

No more talk of dark-ness, for-get these wide-eyed fears; I'm

here, noth-ing can harm you, my words will warm and calm you.

Let me be your free-dom, let day-light dry your tears; I'm

© Copyright 1986 The Really Useful Group Ltd.
All Rights for the United States and Canada Administered by Universal - PolyGram International Publishing, Inc.
International Copyright Secured   All Rights Reserved

here, with you, be-side you, to guard you and to guide you.

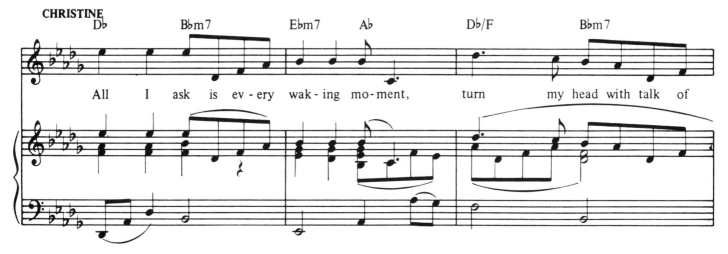

CHRISTINE

All I ask is ev-ery wak-ing mo-ment, turn my head with talk of

sum-mer-time. ___ Say you need me with you now and al-ways;

pro-mise me that all you say is true, that's all I ask of

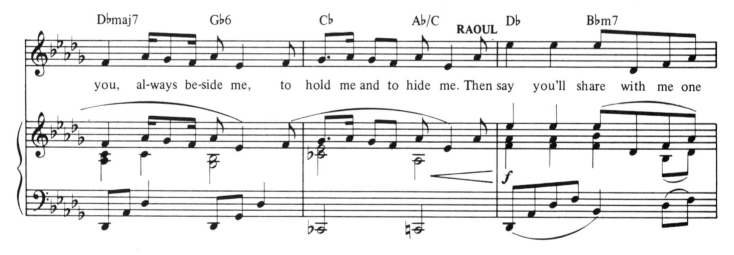

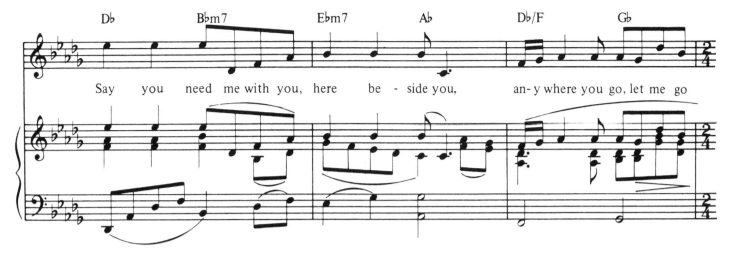

Say you need me with you, here be - side you, an-y where you go, let me go

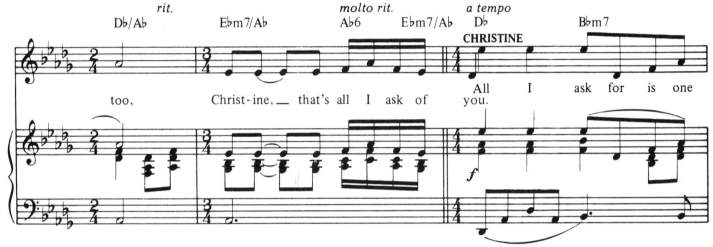

too, Christ-ine, __ that's all I ask of you. All I ask for is one

CHRISTINE

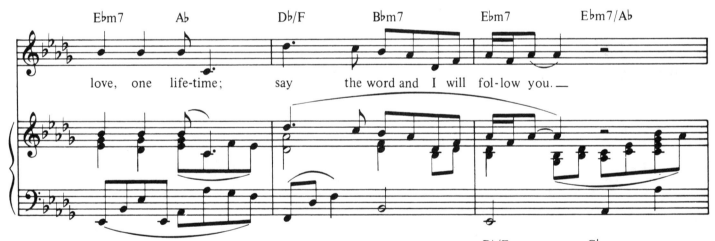

love, one life-time; say the word and I will fol-low you. __

TOGETHER
Share each day with me, each night, each morn-ing.

CHRISTINE
Say you love me!

RAOUL
You know I

6

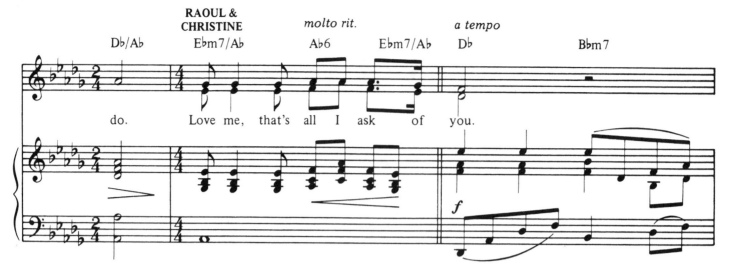

do. Love me, that's all I ask of you.

An-y-where you go, let me go

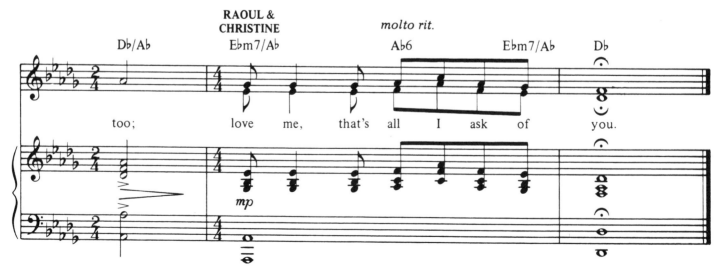

too; love me, that's all I ask of you.

BEWITCHED

from PAL JOEY

Words by LORENZ HART
Music by RICHARD RODGERS

Copyright © 1941 by Williamson Music and The Estate Of Lorenz Hart in the United States
Copyright Renewed
All Rights on behalf of The Estate Of Lorenz Hart Administered by WB Music Corp.
International Copyright Secured   All Rights Reserved

8

ALWAYS

Words and Music by
IRVING BERLIN

Moderate Waltz

Ev - 'ry - thing went wrong,
Dreams will all come true,

and the whole day long _____ I'd feel so
grow - ing old with you, _____ and time will

blue. _____
fly, _____

For the long - est while
car - ing each day more

© Copyright 1925 by Irving Berlin
Copyright Renewed
International Copyright Secured   All Rights Reserved

BLUE SKIES

from BETSY

Words and Music by
IRVING BERLIN

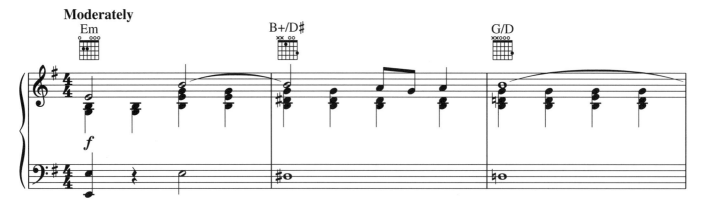

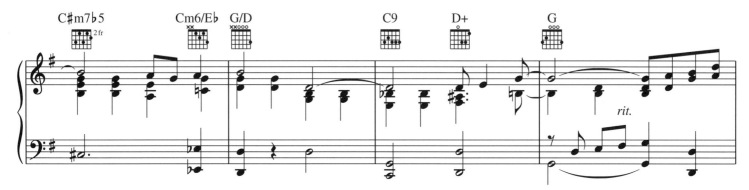

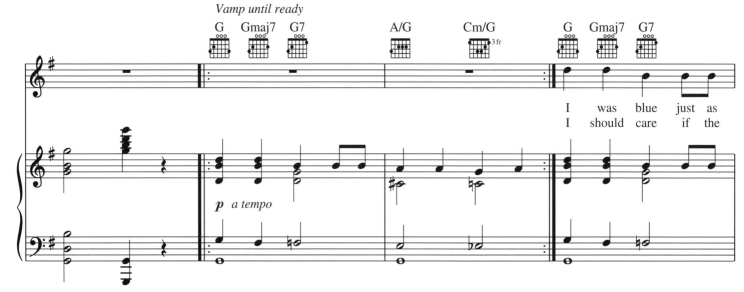

I was blue just as
I should care just if the

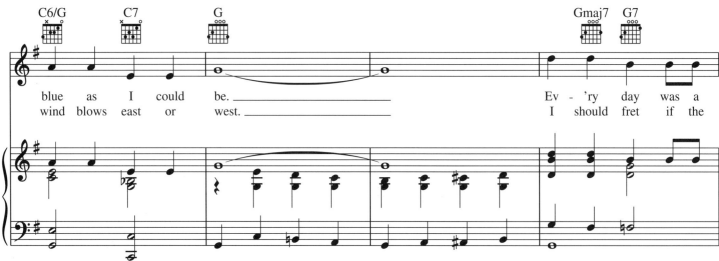

blue as I could be. _____
wind blows east or west. _____

Ev - 'ry day was a
I should fret if the

© Copyright 1927 by Irving Berlin
Copyright Renewed
International Copyright Secured   All Rights Reserved

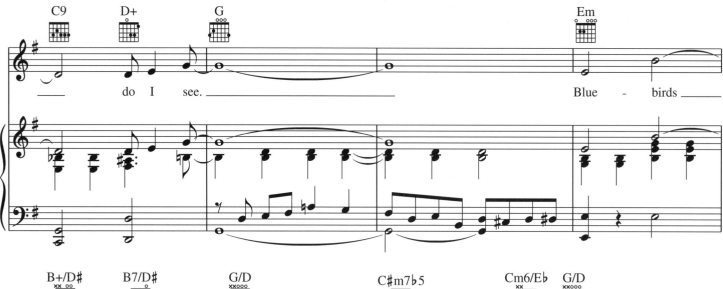

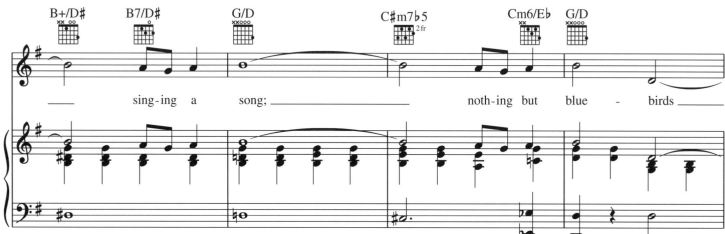

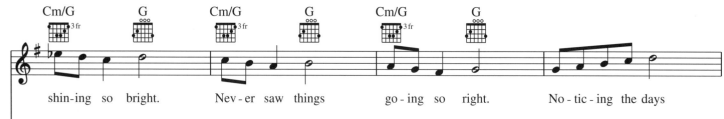

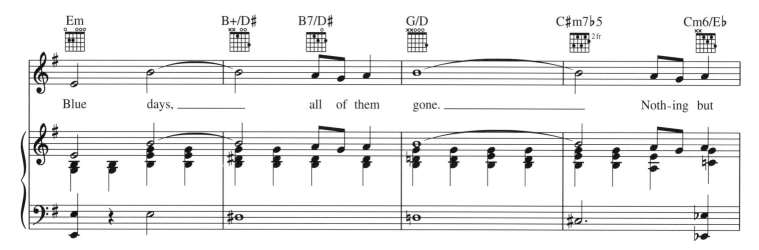

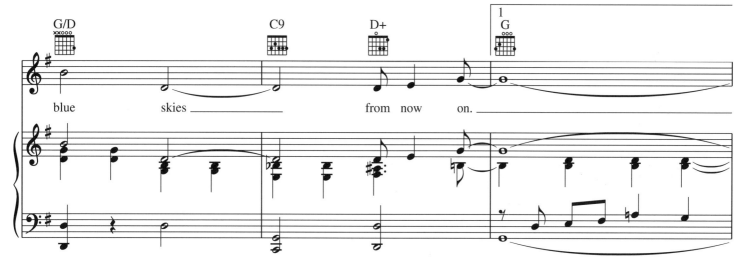

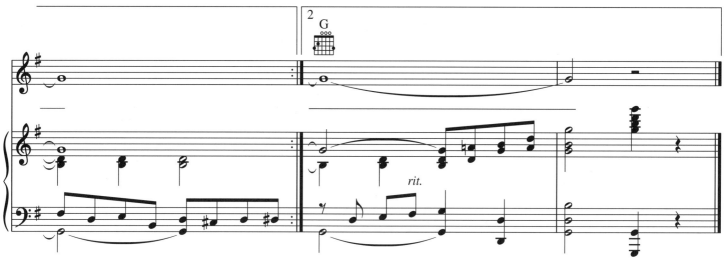

BODY AND SOUL

Words by EDWARD HEYMAN,
ROBERT SOUR and FRANK EYTON
Music by JOHN GREEN

Slow Ballad

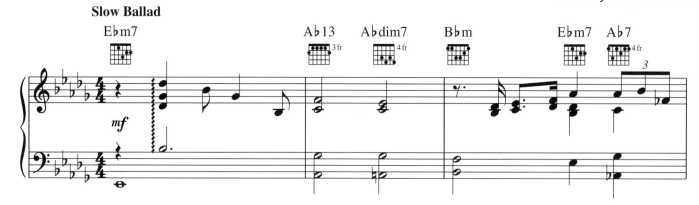

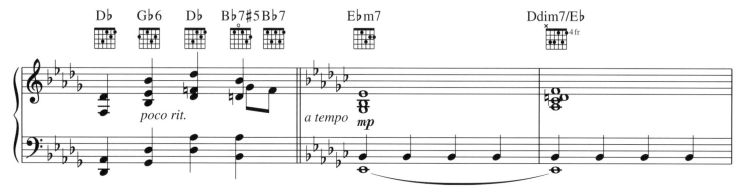

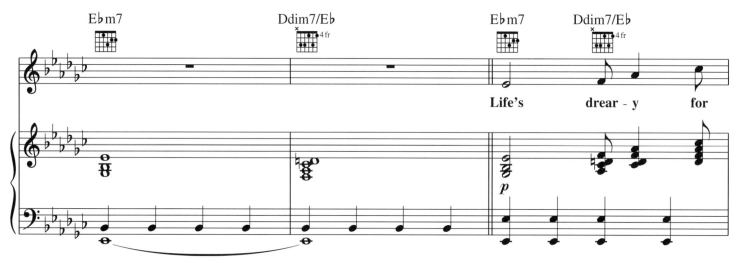

Life's drear-y for

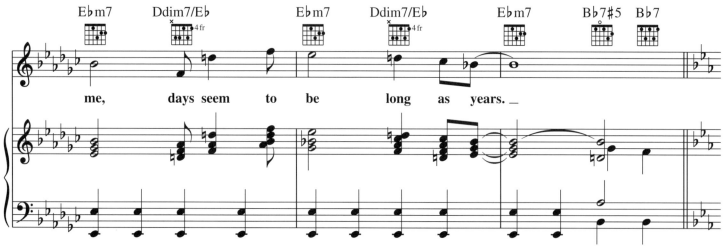

me, days seem to be long as years.

Copyright © 1930 Warner Bros. Inc.
Copyright renewed; extended term of Copyright deriving from Edward Heyman
assigned and effective January 1, 1987 to Range Road Music Inc. and Quartet Music, Inc.
Extended term of Copyright deriving from John Green, Robert Sour and Frank Eyton assigned to Warner Bros. Inc. and Druropetal Music
This arrangement Copyright © 1993 by Range Road Music Inc., Quartet Music Inc., Warner Bros. Inc. and Druropetal Music
International Copyright Secured   All Rights Reserved
Used by Permission

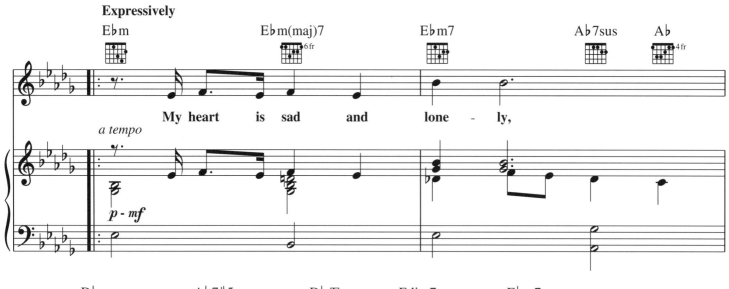

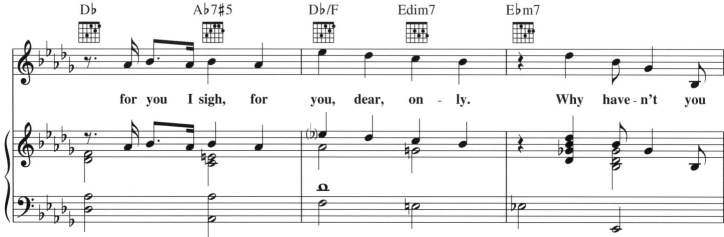

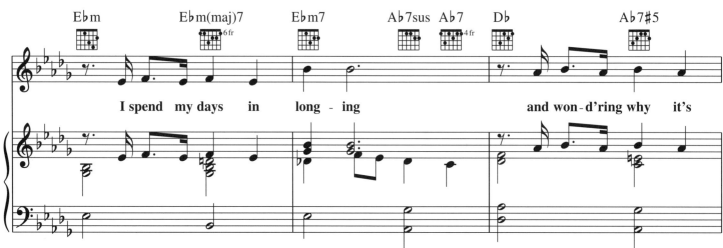

me you're wrong - ing, I tell you I mean it,

I'm all for you, bod - y and soul! I can't be - lieve it, it's

hard to con - ceive it that you'd turn a - way ro - mance.___

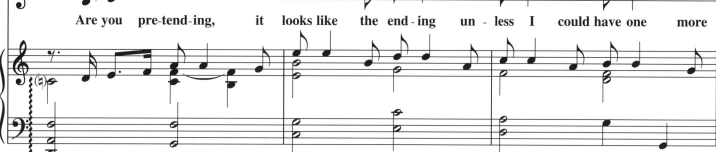

Are you pre - tend - ing, it looks like the end - ing un - less I could have one more

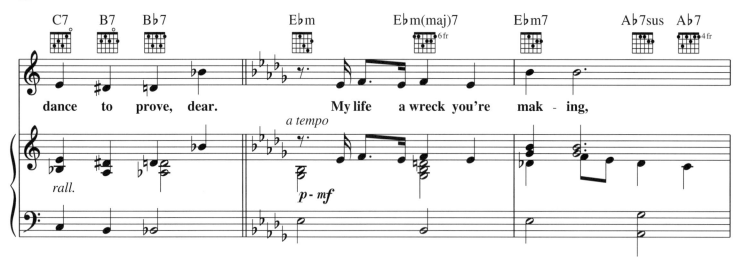

dance to prove, dear. My life a wreck you're mak - ing,

you know I'm yours for just the tak - ing; I'd glad - ly sur -

ren - der my - self to you, bod - y and

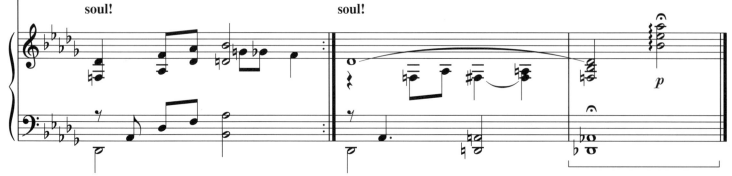

soul!

soul!

CAN'T HELP FALLING IN LOVE

from the Paramount Picture BLUE HAWAII

Words and Music by GEORGE DAVID WEISS,
HUGO PERETTI and LUIGI CREATORE

Wise men say on-ly fools rush in, _____ but I can't help fall-ing in love with you. Shall I

Copyright © 1961 by Gladys Music, Inc.
Copyright Renewed and Assigned to Gladys Music (Administered by Williamson Music)
International Copyright Secured   All Rights Reserved

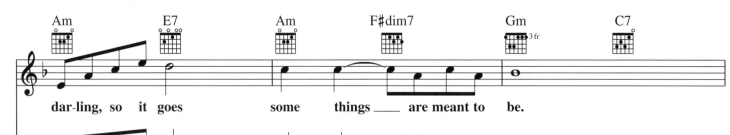

CALL ME IRRESPONSIBLE

from the Paramount Picture PAPA'S DELICATE CONDITION

Words by SAMMY CAHN
Music by JAMES VAN HEUSEN

Copyright © 1962, 1963 (Renewed 1990, 1991) by Paramount Music Corporation
International Copyright Secured   All Rights Reserved

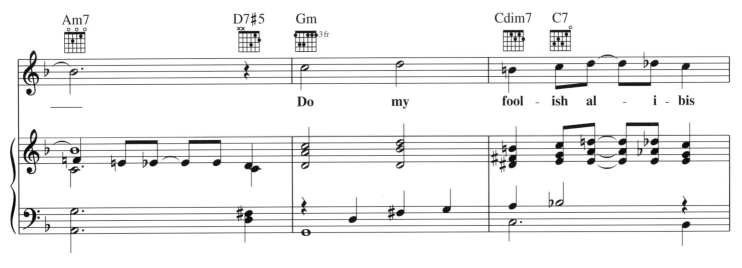

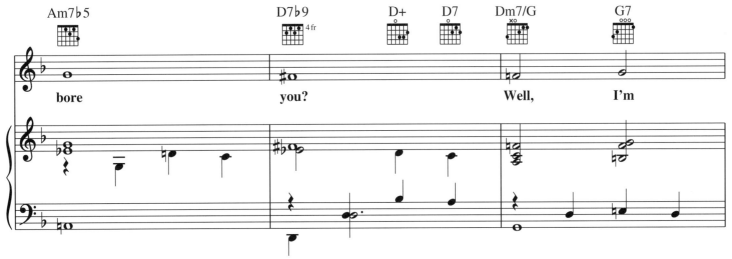

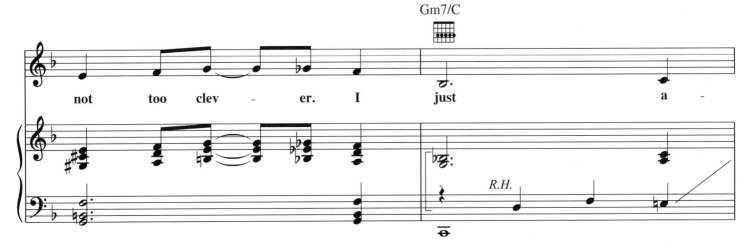

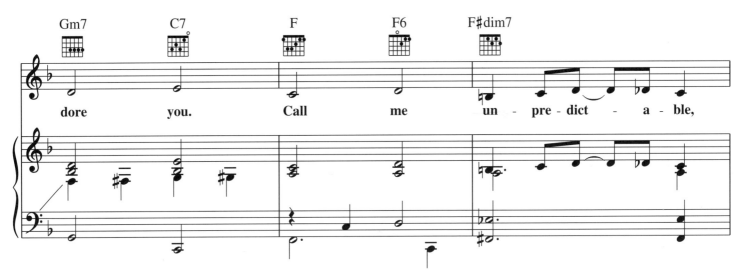

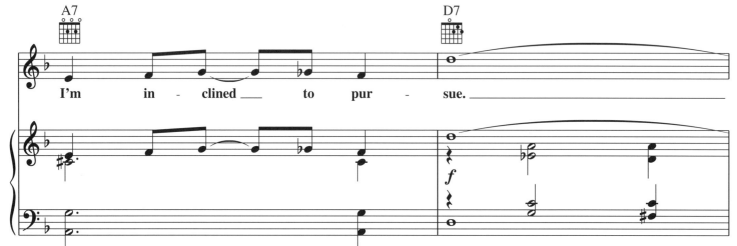

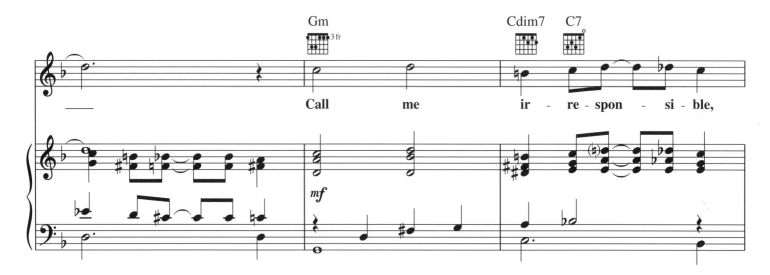

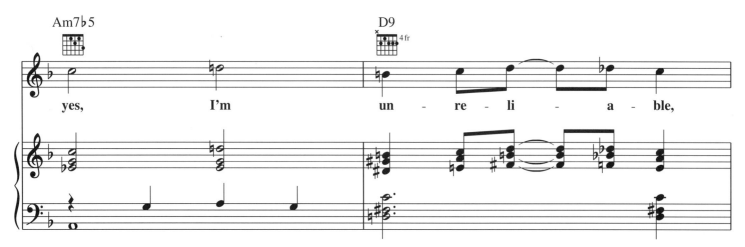

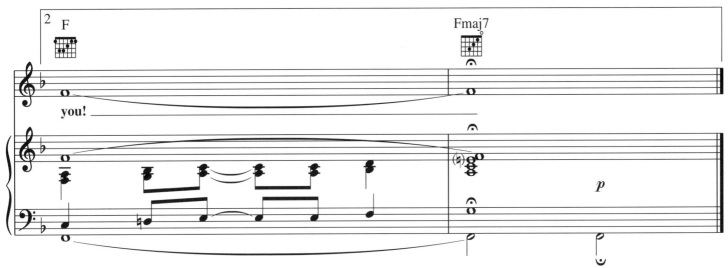

CAN YOU FEEL THE LOVE TONIGHT

from Walt Disney Pictures' THE LION KING

Music by ELTON JOHN
Lyrics by TIM RICE

© 1994 Wonderland Music Company, Inc.
All Rights Reserved   Used by Permission

31

wide - eyed ___ wan-der-er   that we got this far. __

__ And can you feel __ the love __

__ to - night, ____ how it's laid ___ to rest? __

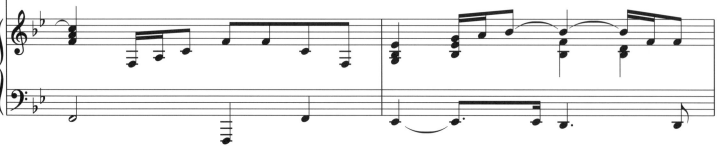

__ It's e - nough _____ to make

kings ___ and ___ vag-a-bonds ___ be-lieve the ver - y best. ___

It's e-nough ___ to make

kings ___ and ___ vag-a-bonds ___ be-lieve the ver - y best. ___

CHARIOTS OF FIRE

from CHARIOTS OF FIRE

Music by VANGELIS

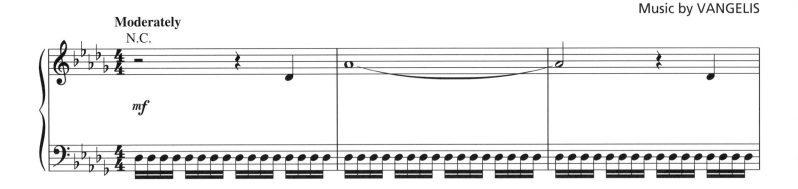

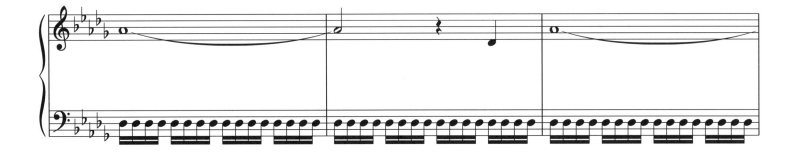

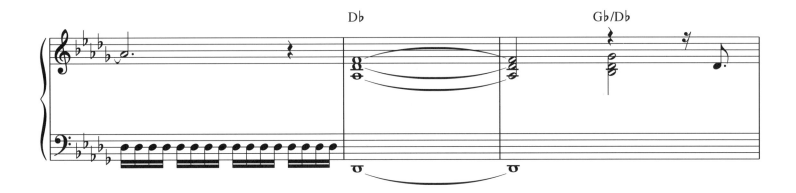

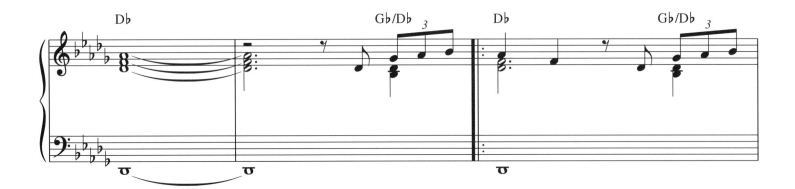

© 1981 EMI MUSIC PUBLISHING LTD.
All Rights for the World, excluding Holland, Controlled and Administered by EMI APRIL MUSIC INC.
All Rights Reserved   International Copyright Secured   Used by Permission

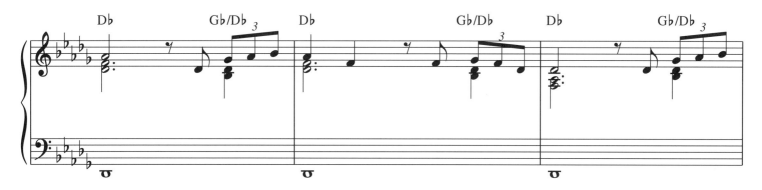

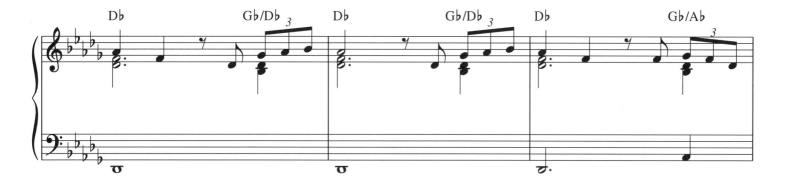

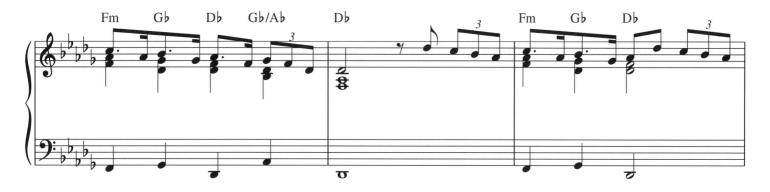

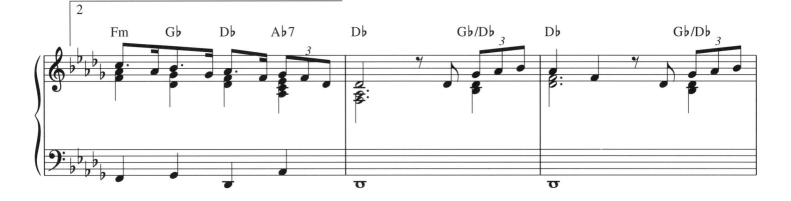

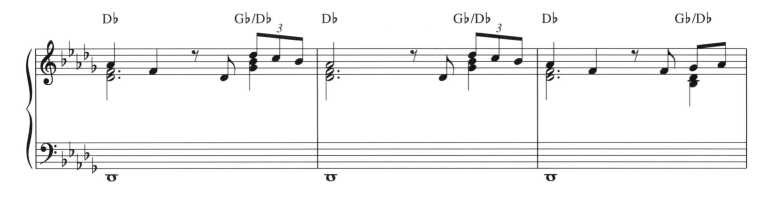

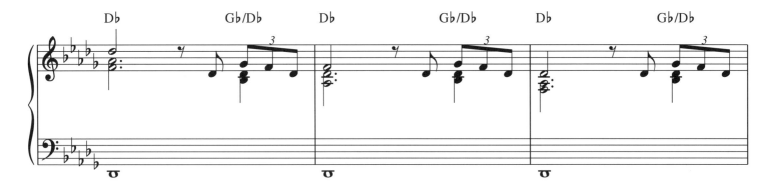

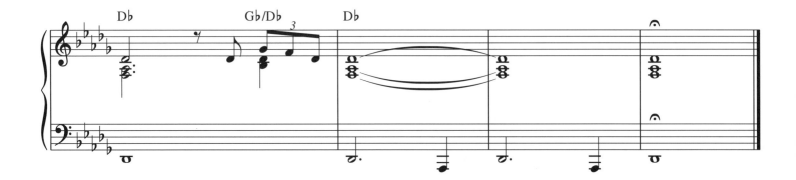

CLIMB EV'RY MOUNTAIN
from THE SOUND OF MUSIC

Lyrics by OSCAR HAMMERSTEIN II
Music by RICHARD RODGERS

Maestoso

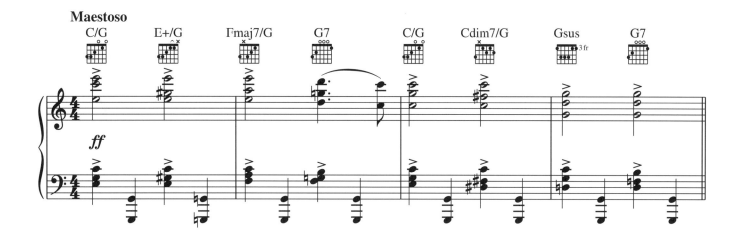

Refrain (*with deep feeling, like a prayer*)

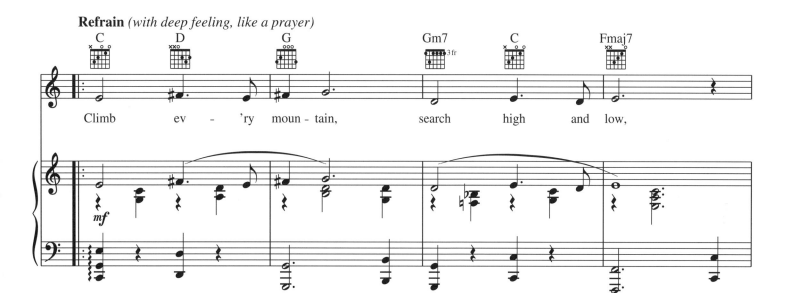

Climb ev-'ry moun-tain, search high and low,

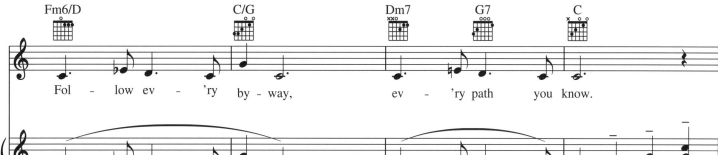

Fol-low ev-'ry by-way, ev-'ry path you know.

Copyright © 1959 by Richard Rodgers and Oscar Hammerstein II
Copyright Renewed
WILLIAMSON MUSIC owner of publication and allied rights throughout the world
International Copyright Secured   All Rights Reserved

38

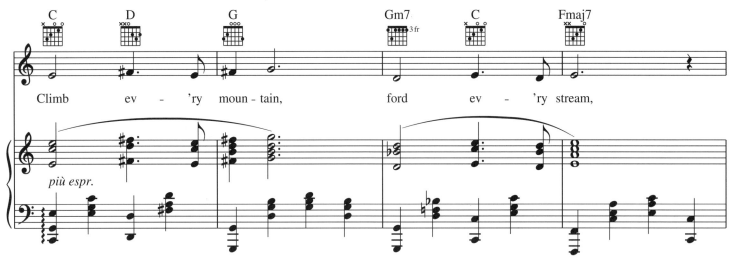

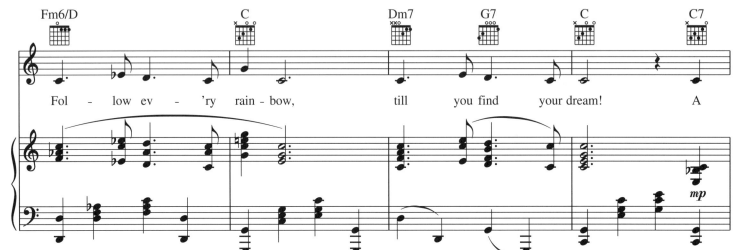

CRAZY

Words and Music by
WILLIE NELSON

Moderately slow

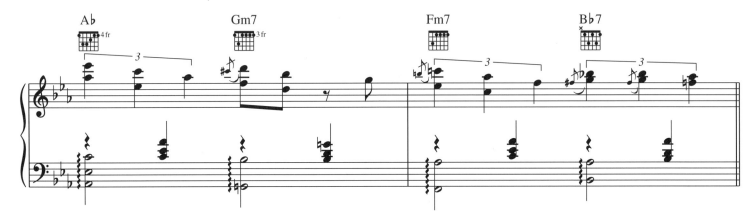

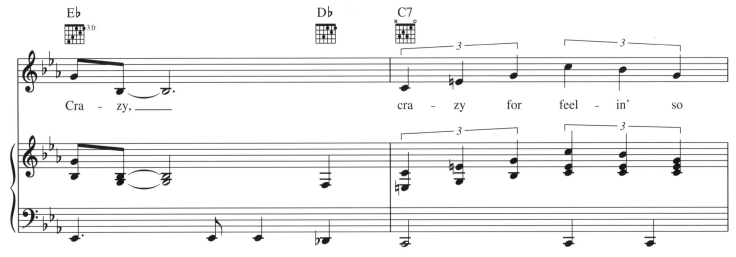

Cra - zy, _____ cra - zy for feel - in' so

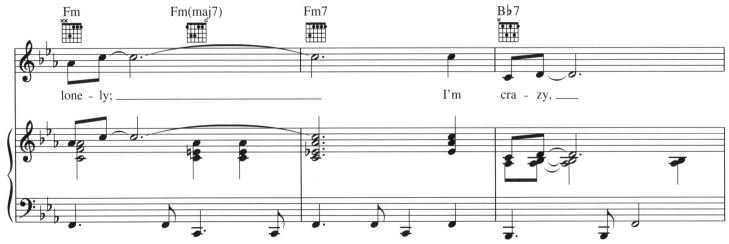

lone - ly; _____ I'm cra - zy, ___

Copyright © 1961 Sony/ATV Songs LLC
Copyright Renewed
All Rights Administered by Sony/ATV Music Publishing, 8 Music Square West, Nashville, TN 37203
International Copyright Secured   All Rights Reserved

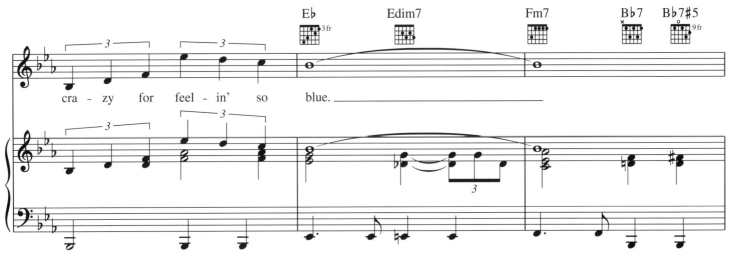

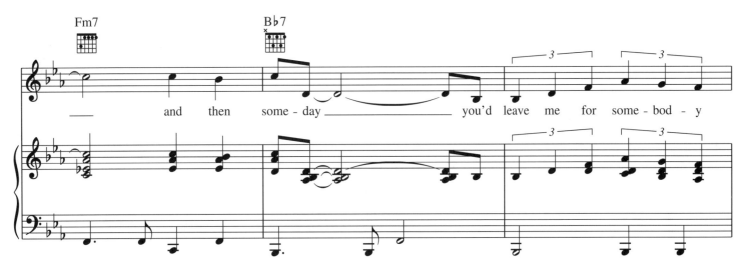

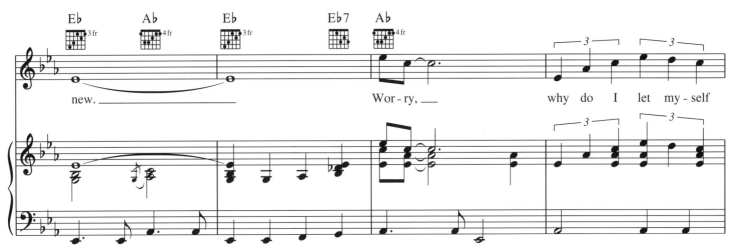

EDELWEISS
from THE SOUND OF MUSIC

Lyrics by OSCAR HAMMERSTEIN II
Music by RICHARD RODGERS

Copyright © 1959 by Richard Rodgers and Oscar Hammerstein II
Copyright Renewed
WILLIAMSON MUSIC owner of publication and allied rights throughout the world
International Copyright Secured   All Rights Reserved

FLY ME TO THE MOON
(In Other Words)

Words and Music by
BART HOWARD

TRO - © Copyright 1954 (Renewed) Hampshire House Publishing Corp., New York, NY
International Copyright Secured
All Rights Reserved Including Public Performance For Profit
Used by Permission

47

FROM A DISTANCE

Words and Music by
JULIE GOLD

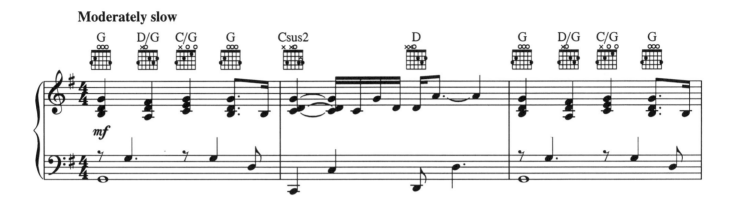

Moderately slow

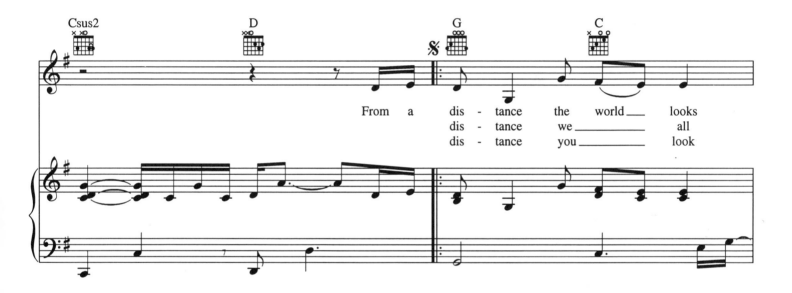

From a dis - tance the world ___ looks
dis - tance we ___ all
dis - tance you ___ look

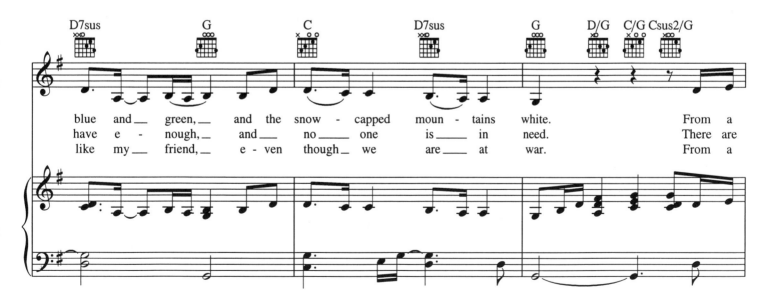

blue and ___ green, ___ and the snow - capped moun - tains white. From a
have e - nough, ___ and ___ no ___ one is ___ in need. There are
like my ___ friend, ___ e - ven though ___ we are ___ at war. From a

Copyright © 1986, 1987 Julie Gold Music (BMI) and Wing & Wheel Music (BMI)
Julie Gold Music Administered Worldwide by Cherry River Music Co.
Wing & Wheel Music Administered Worldwide by Irving Music, Inc.
International Copyright Secured   All Rights Reserved

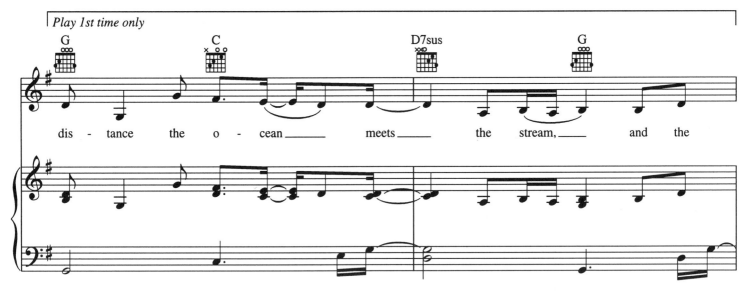

Play 1st time only

dis - tance the o - cean _____ meets _____ the stream, _____ and the

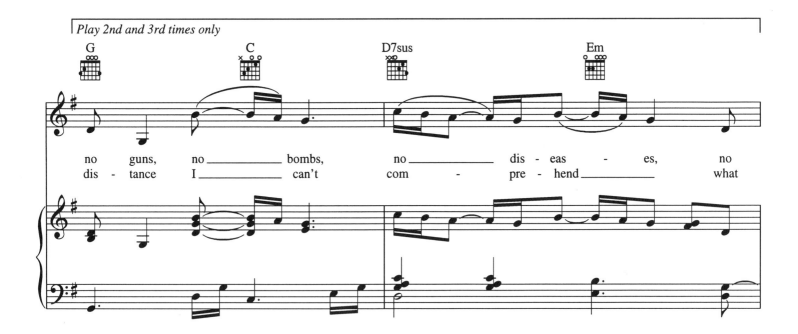

Play 2nd and 3rd times only

no guns, no _____ bombs, no _____ dis - eas - es, no
dis - tance I _____ can't com - pre - hend _____ what

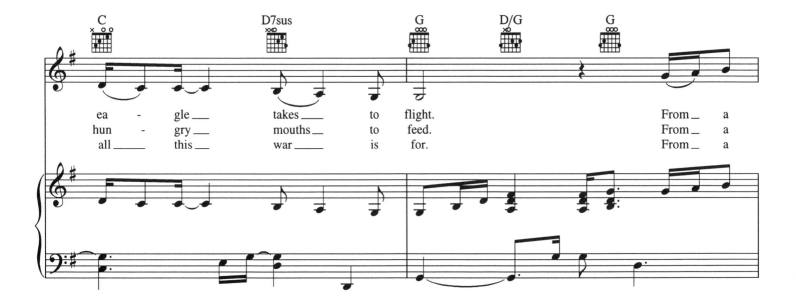

ea - gle _____ takes _____ to flight. From __ a
hun - gry _____ mouths _____ to feed. From __ a
all _____ this _____ war _____ is for. From __ a

dis - tance there _____ is har - mo - ny, and it _____
dis - tance we _____ are in - stru - ments, march - ing _____
dis - tance there _____ is har - mo - ny, and it _____

ech - oes through _____ the land. _____ It's the
in a com - mon band. _____ Play - ing
ech - oes through _____ the land. _____ It's the

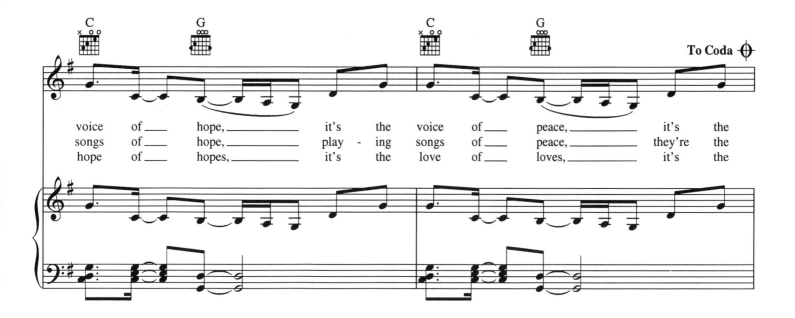

voice of _____ hope, _____ it's the voice of _____ peace, _____ it's the
songs of _____ hope, _____ play - ing songs of _____ peace, _____ they're the
hope of _____ hopes, _____ it's the love of _____ loves, _____ it's the

To Coda ⊕

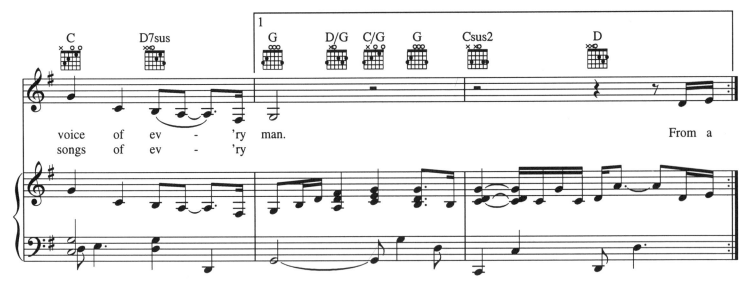

voice   of   ev - 'ry   man.   From a
songs   of   ev - 'ry

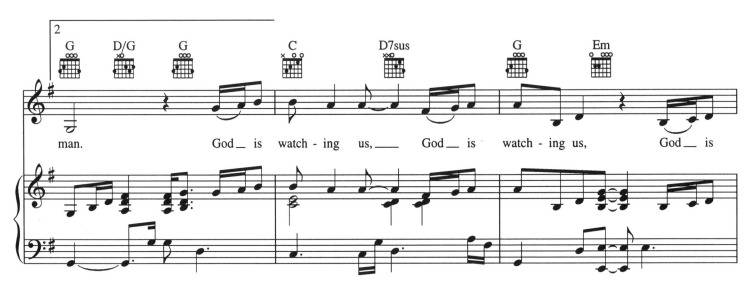

man.   God __ is   watch - ing   us, ___   God __ is   watch - ing   us,   God __ is

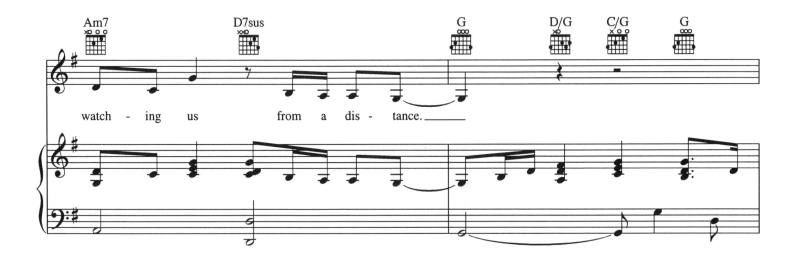

watch - ing   us   from   a   dis - tance. _____

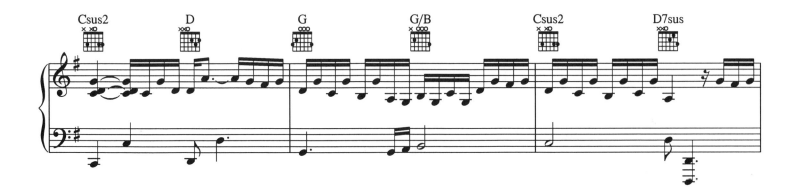

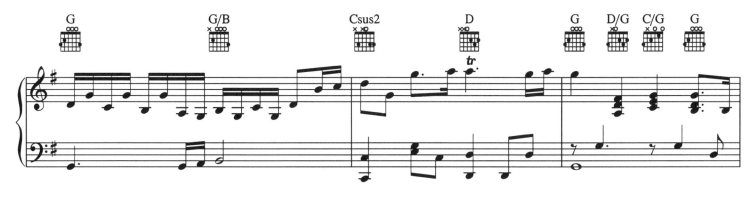

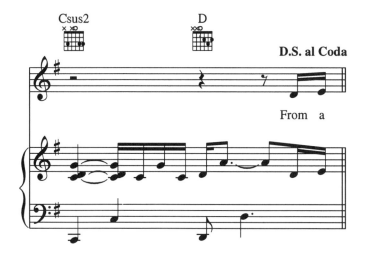
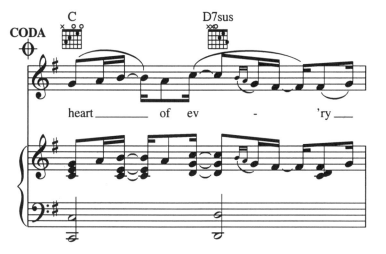

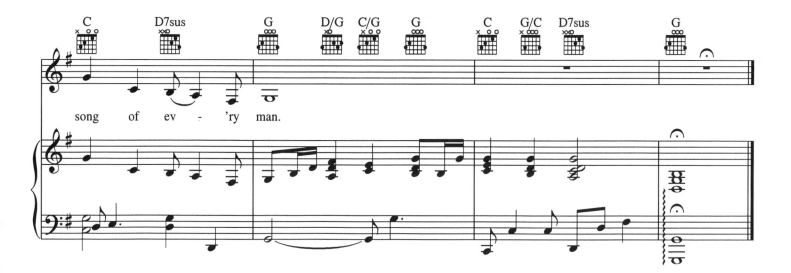

GEORGIA ON MY MIND

Words by STUART GORRELL
Music by HOAGY CARMICHAEL

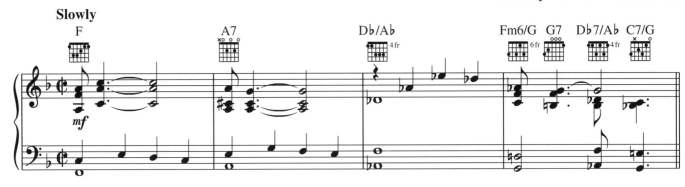

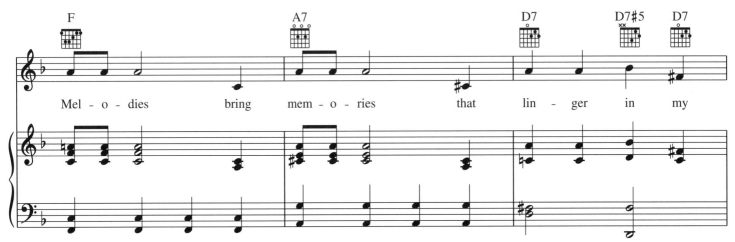

Mel - o - dies bring mem - o - ries that lin - ger in my

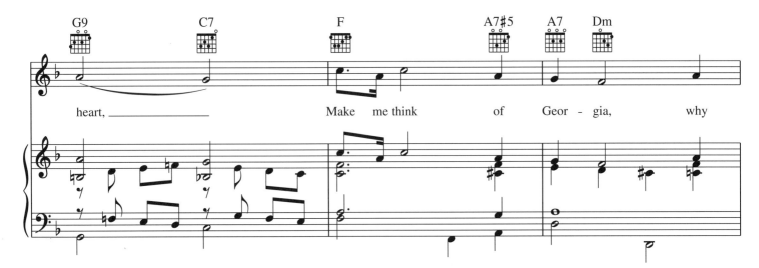

heart, _____ Make me think of Geor - gia, why

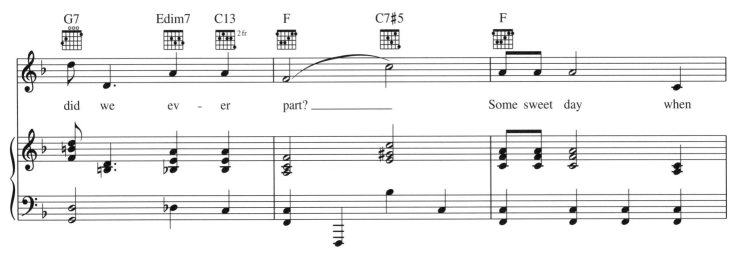

did we ev - er part? _____ Some sweet day when

Copyright © 1930 by Peermusic Ltd.
Copyright Renewed
International Copyright Secured   All Rights Reserved

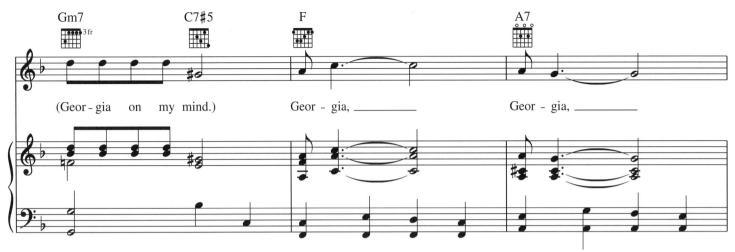

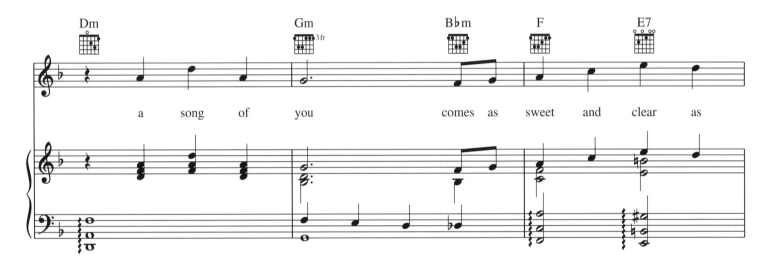

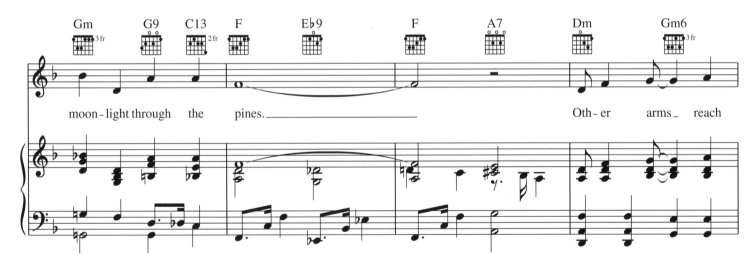

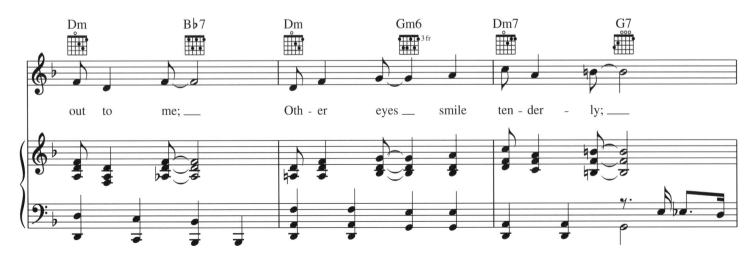

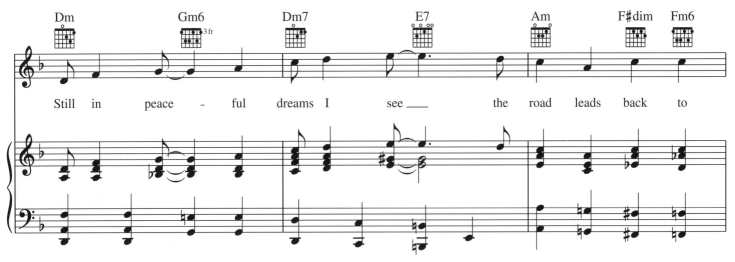

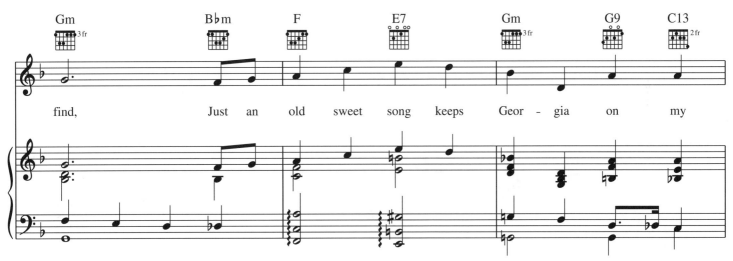

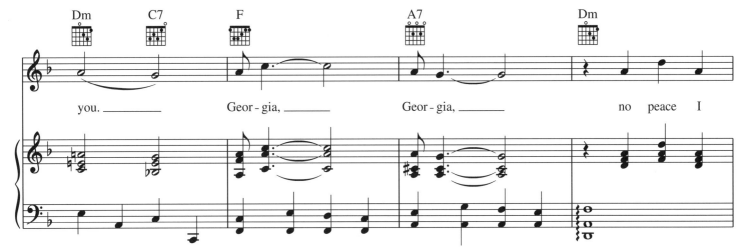

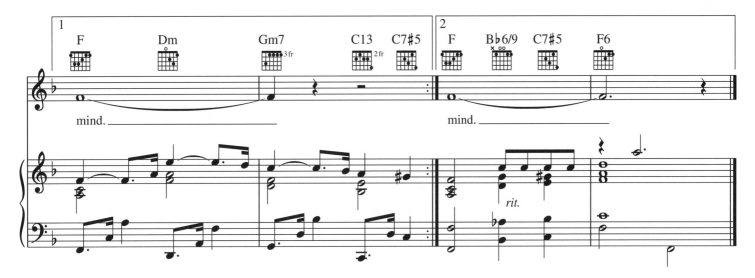

HERE'S THAT RAINY DAY
from CARNIVAL IN FLANDERS

Words by JOHNNY BURKE
Music by JIMMY VAN HEUSEN

Very Slow

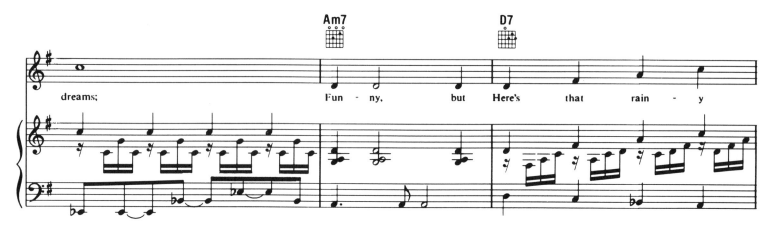

Copyright © 1953 by Bourne Co. and Music Sales Corporation (ASCAP)
Copyright Renewed
International Copyright Secured   All Rights Reserved
Reprinted by Permission

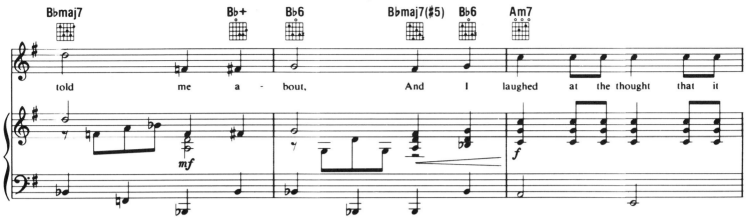

told me a - bout, And I laughed at the thought that it

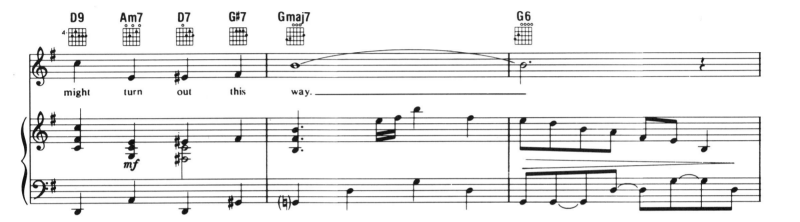

might turn out this way. _____

Where is that worn out wish that I threw a -

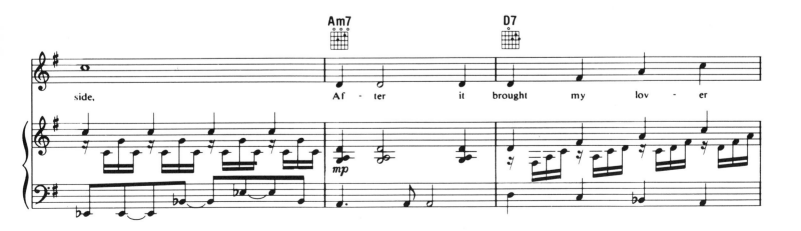

side, After it brought my lov - er

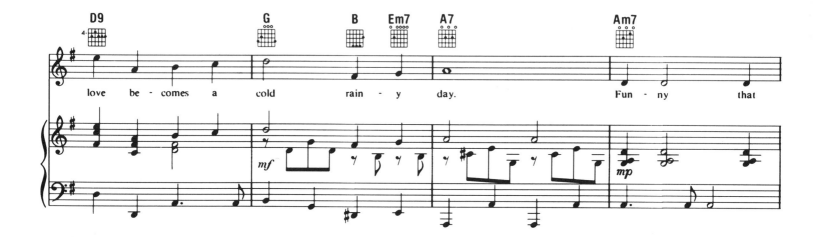

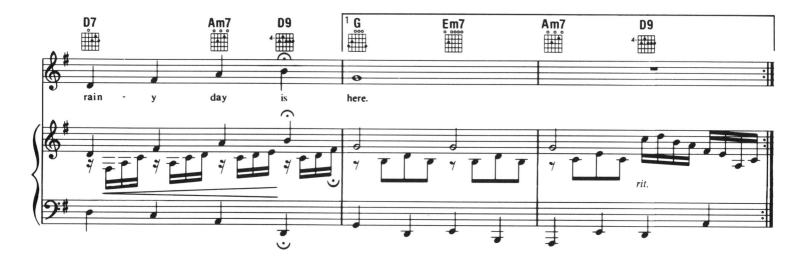

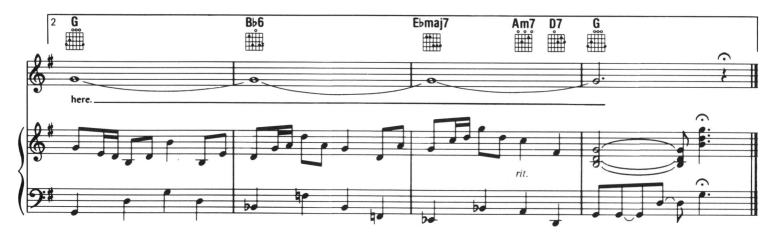

HOW DEEP IS THE OCEAN
(How High Is the Sky)

Words and Music by
IRVING BERLIN

© Copyright 1932 by Irving Berlin
Copyright Renewed
International Copyright Secured All Rights Reserved

I LEFT MY HEART IN SAN FRANCISCO

Words by DOUGLASS CROSS
Music by GEORGE CORY

© 1954 (Renewed 1982) COLGEMS-EMI MUSIC INC.
All Rights Reserved   International Copyright Secured   Used by Permission

ISN'T IT ROMANTIC?

from the Paramount Picture LOVE ME TONIGHT

Words by LORENZ HART
Music by RICHARD RODGERS

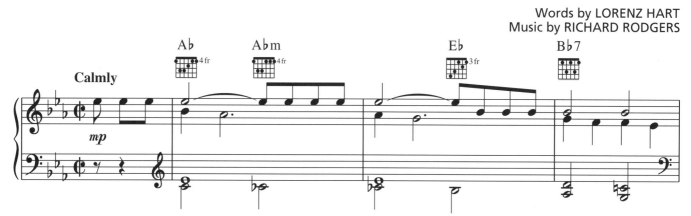

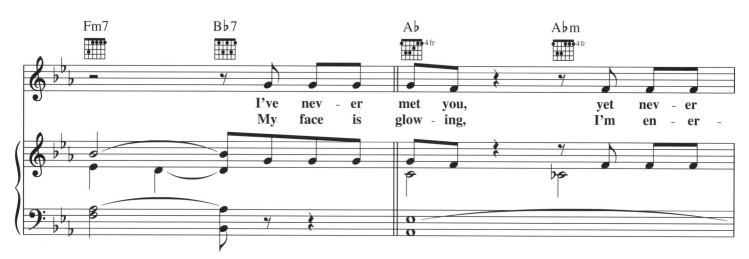

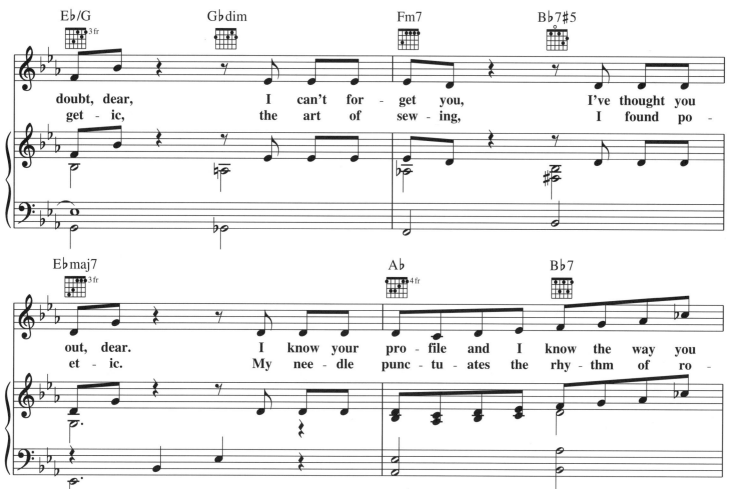

I've nev-er met you, yet nev-er
My face is glow-ing, I'm en-er-

doubt, dear, I can't for-get you, I've thought you
get-ic, the art of sew-ing, I found po-

out, dear. I know your pro-file and I know the way you
et-ic. My nee-dle punc-tu-ates the rhy-thm of ro-

Copyright © 1932 (Renewed 1959) by Famous Music Corporation
International Copyright Secured   All Rights Reserved

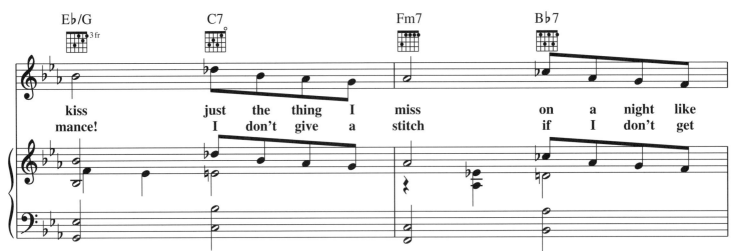

kiss   just the thing I miss   on a night like

mance!   I don't give a stitch   if I don't get

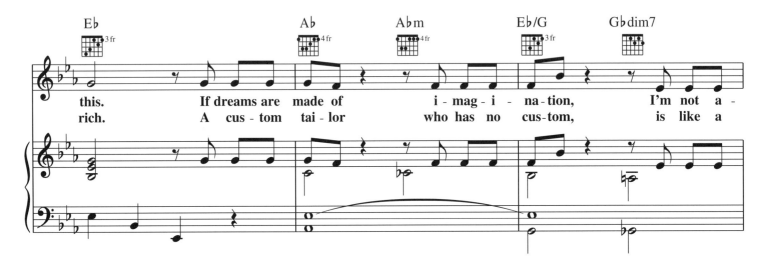

this.   If dreams are made of   i - mag - i - na - tion,   I'm not a -

rich.   A cus - tom tai - lor   who has no cus - tom,   is like a

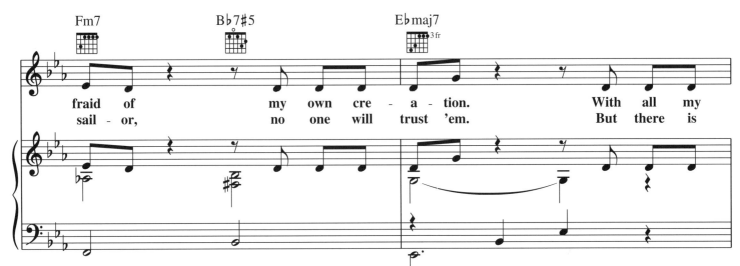

fraid of   my own cre - a - tion.   With all my

sail - or,   no one will trust 'em.   But there is

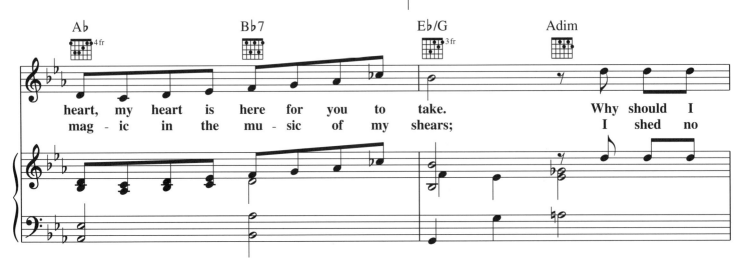

heart, my heart is here for you to take.   Why should I

mag - ic in the mu - sic of my shears;   I shed no

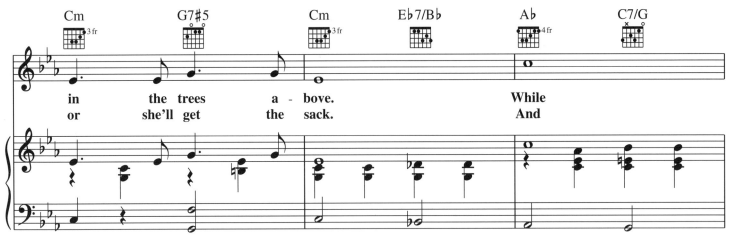

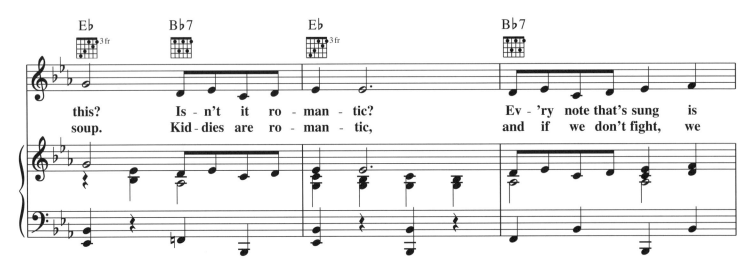

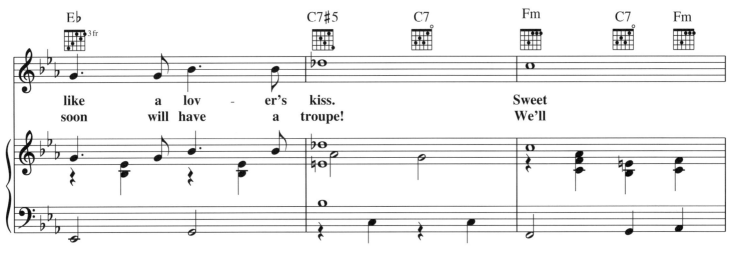

like a lov - er's kiss. Sweet
soon will have a troupe! We'll

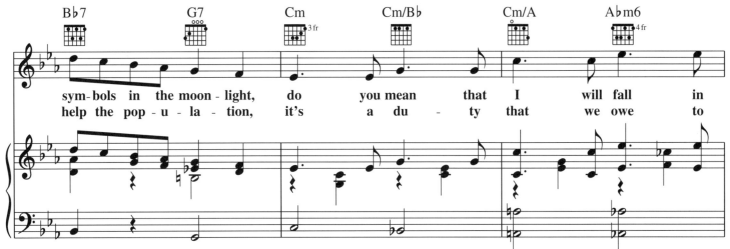

sym - bols in the moon - light, do you mean that I will fall in
help the pop - u - la - tion, it's a du - ty that we owe to

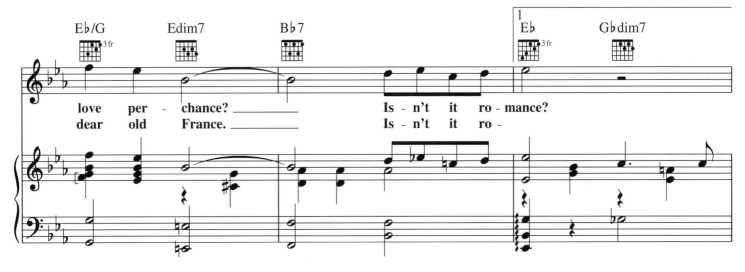

love per - chance? _____ Is - n't it ro - mance?
dear old France. _____ Is - n't it ro -

Is - n't it ro - mance? _____

I WRITE THE SONGS

Words and Music by
BRUCE JOHNSTON

Copyright © 1970 by Artists Music, Inc.
Copyright Renewed
All Rights Administered by BMG Songs, Inc.
International Copyright Secured   All Rights Reserved

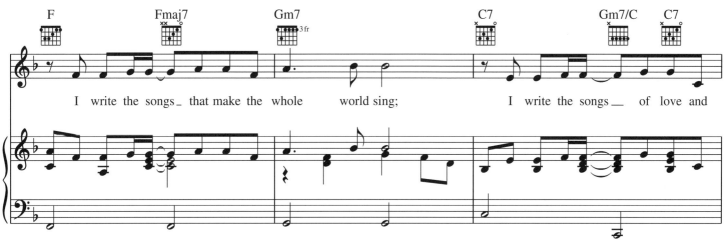

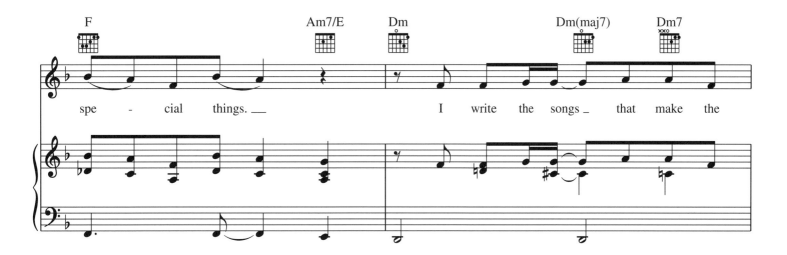

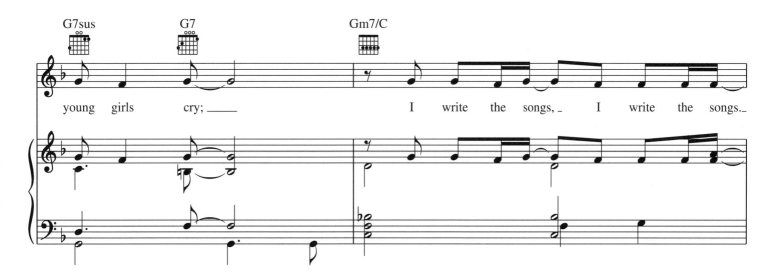

I'LL BE SEEING YOU

from RIGHT THIS WAY

Lyric by IRVING KAHAL
Music by SAMMY FAIN

Copyright © 1938 The New Irving Kahal Music Company and Fain Music Co.
Copyright Renewed
All Rights for The New Irving Kahal Music Company Administered by Fred Ahlert Music Corporation
International Copyright Secured   All Rights Reserved

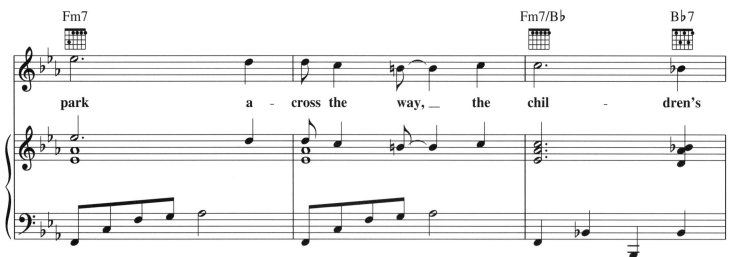

park a - cross the way, __ the chil - dren's

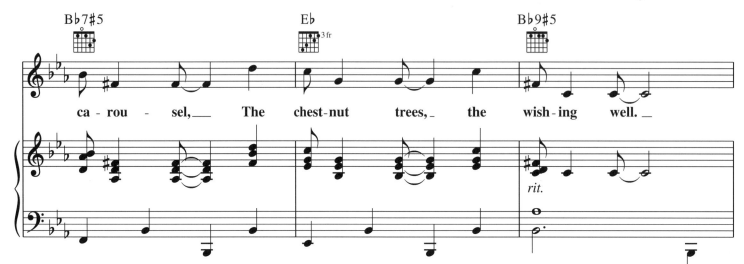

ca - rou - sel, __ The chest - nut trees, __ the wish - ing well. __

rit.

I'll be see - ing you __ In ev - 'ry love - ly

a tempo

sum - mer's day, In ev - 'ry - thing that's light and gay, I'll

al - ways think of you that way I'll find you in the

morn - ing sun; And when the night is new, I'll be

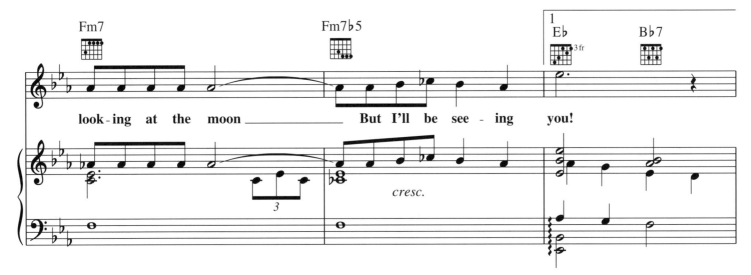

look - ing at the moon _____ But I'll be see - ing you!

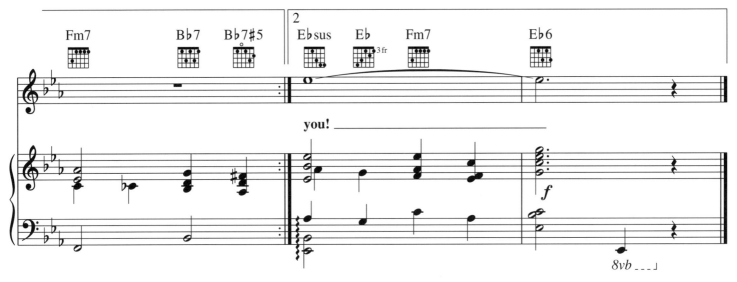

you! _____

IMAGINE

Words and Music by
JOHN LENNON

© 1971 (Renewed 1999) LENONO.MUSIC
All Rights Controlled and Administered by EMI BLACKWOOD MUSIC INC.
All Rights Reserved   International Copyright Secured   Used by Permission

IT MIGHT AS WELL BE SPRING

from STATE FAIR

Lyrics by OSCAR HAMMERSTEIN II
Music by RICHARD RODGERS

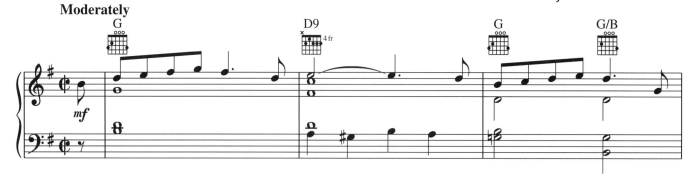

The things I used to like I don't like an-y-more. I want a lot of oth-er things I've

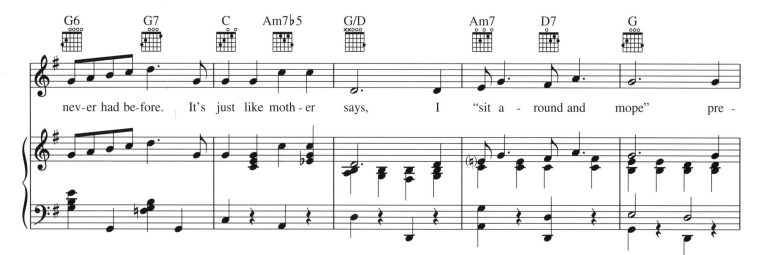

nev-er had be-fore. It's just like moth-er says, I "sit a-round and mope" pre-

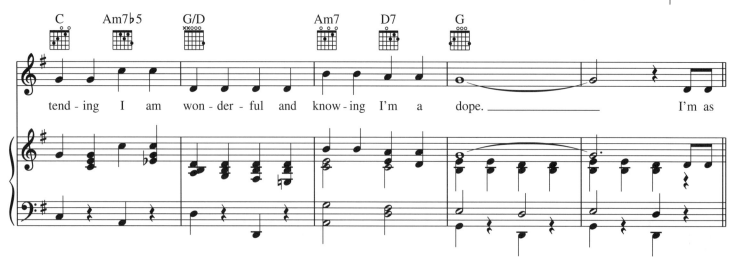

tend-ing I am won-der-ful and know-ing I'm a dope. _____ I'm as

Copyright © 1945 by WILLIAMSON MUSIC
Copyright Renewed
International Copyright Secured All Rights Reserved

rest-less as a wil-low in a wind-storm. I'm as jump-y as a pup-pet on a string. I'd

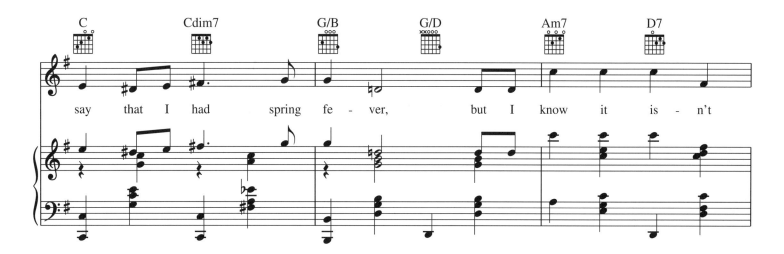

say that I had spring fe - ver, but I know it is - n't

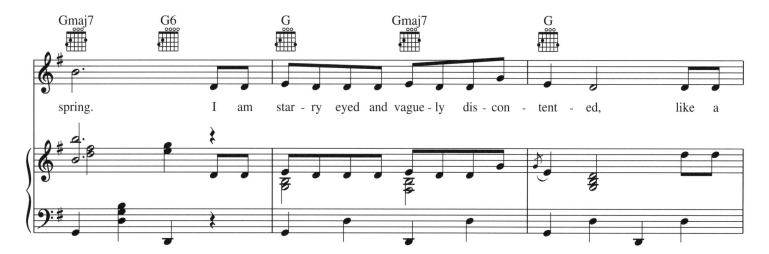

spring. I am star-ry eyed and vague-ly dis-con - tent - ed, like a

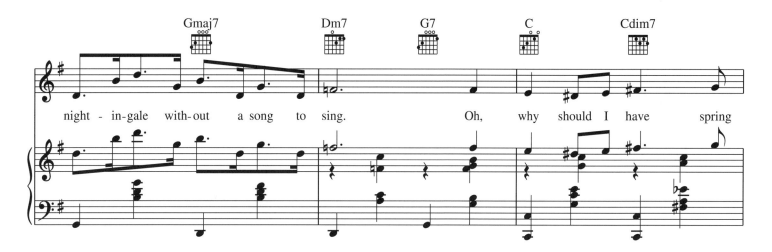

night-in-gale with-out a song to sing. Oh, why should I have spring

fe - ver when it is - n't e - ven spring? I keep wish-ing I were

some - where else, walk-ing down a strange new street, hear - ing words that I have

nev - er heard from a {man/girl} I've yet to meet. I'm as

bus - y as a spi - der spin-ning day-dreams, I'm as gid - dy as a ba - by on a

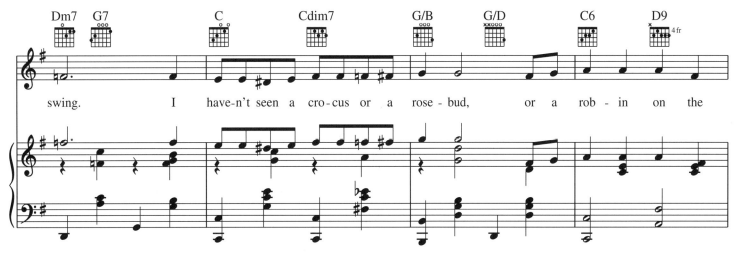

swing. I have-n't seen a cro-cus or a rose-bud, or a rob-in on the

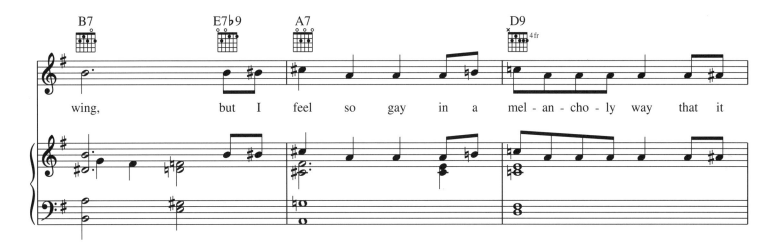

wing, but I feel so gay in a mel - an - cho - ly way that it

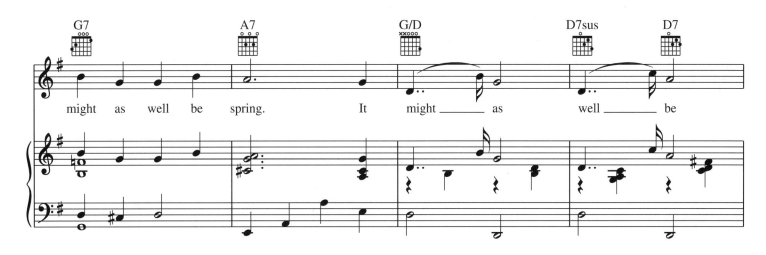

might as well be spring. It might _____ as well _____ be

spring! I'm as spring! _____

JUST THE WAY YOU ARE

Words and Music by
BILLY JOEL

© 1977, 1978 IMPULSIVE MUSIC
All Rights Reserved   International Copyright Secured   Used by Permission

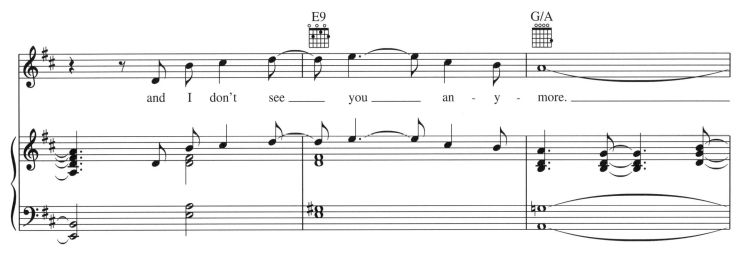

and I don't see ___ you ___ an - y - more. ___

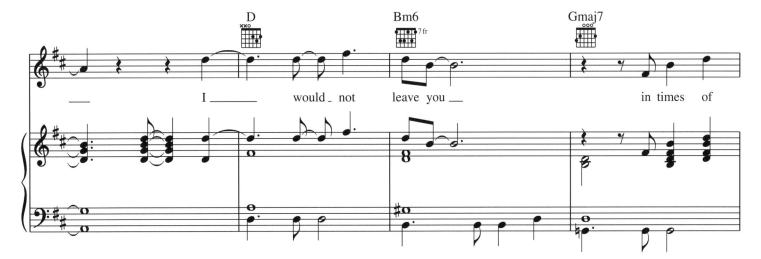

___ I ___ would not leave you ___ in times of

trou - ble. ___ We nev - er could have come ___ this far. ___

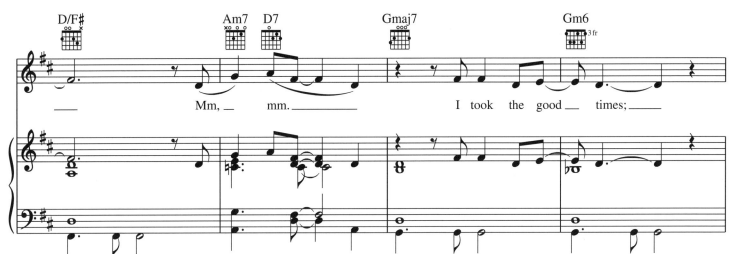

___ Mm, ___ mm. ___ I took the good ___ times; ___

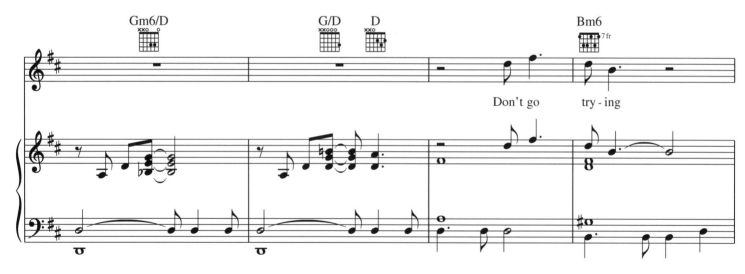

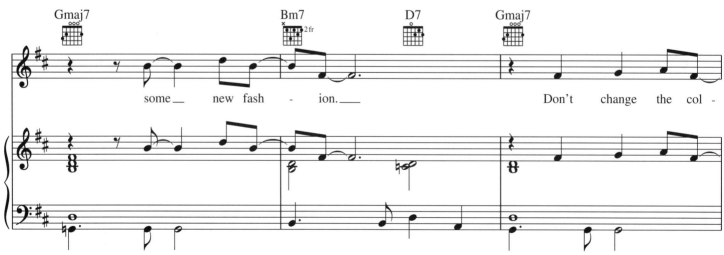

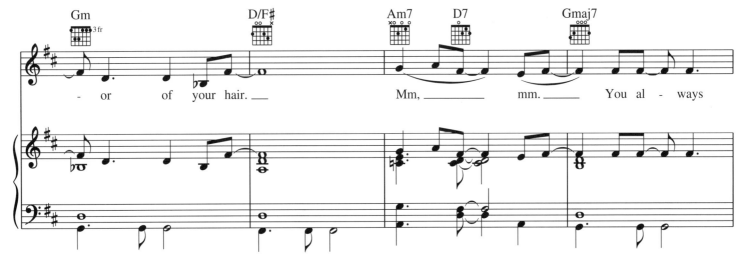

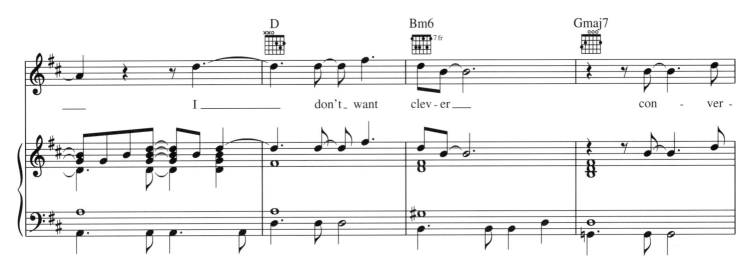

94

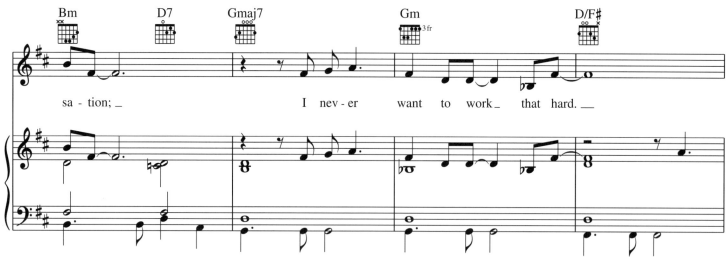

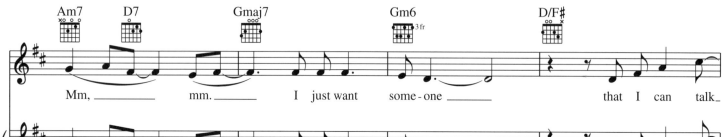

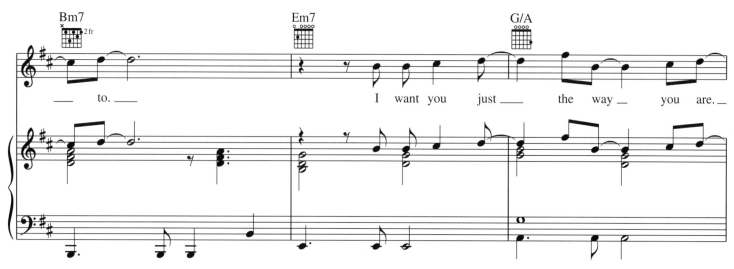

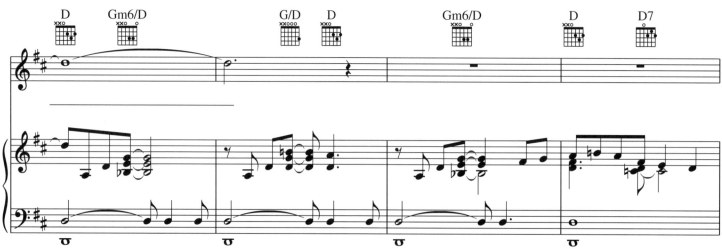

I need to know _ that you _ will al - ways be _

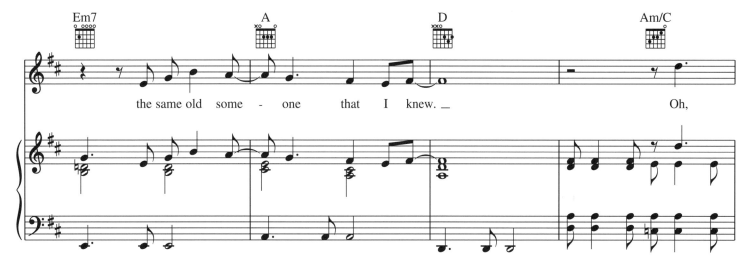

the same old some - one that I knew. _ Oh,

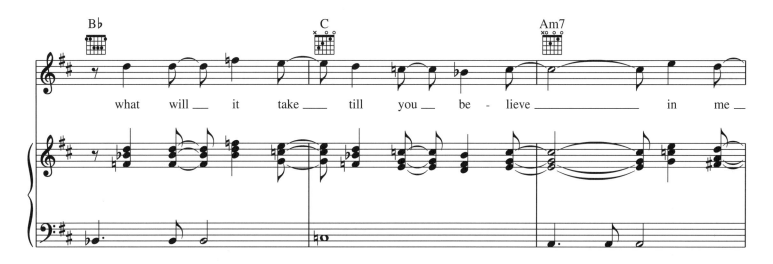

what will _ it take _ till you _ be - lieve _____ in me _

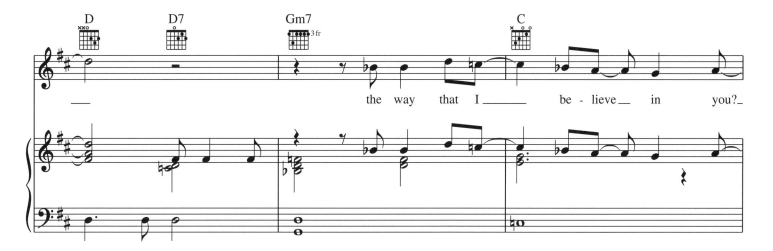

_ the way that I _____ be - lieve _ in you? _

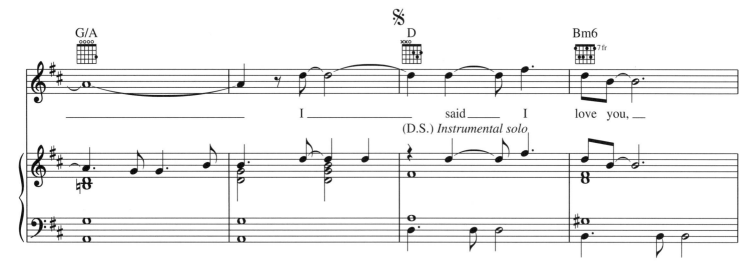

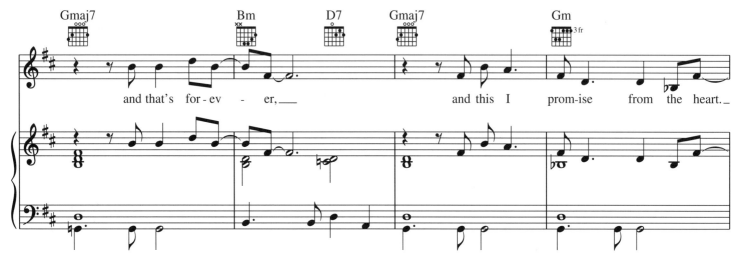

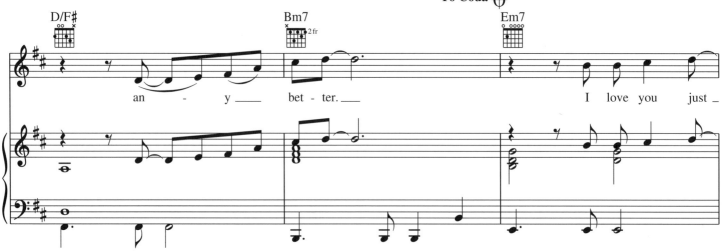

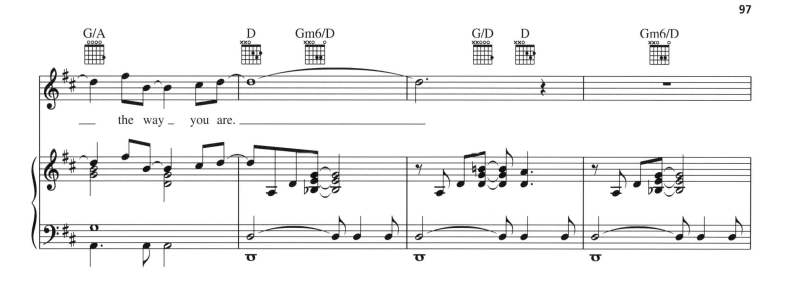

the way you are.

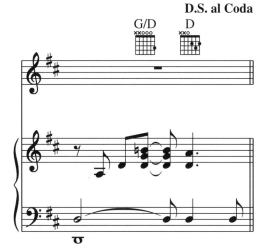

D.S. al Coda

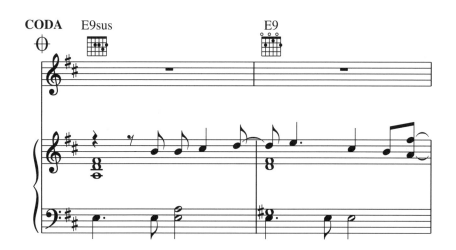

CODA

Solo ends

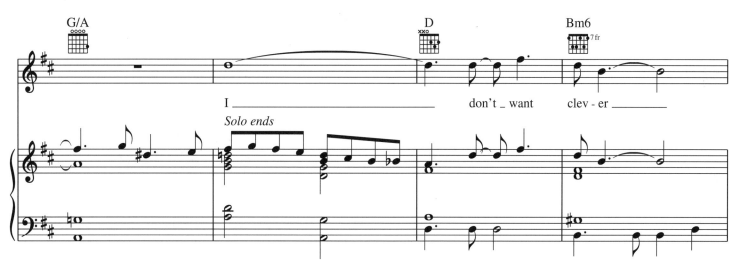

I don't want clev-er

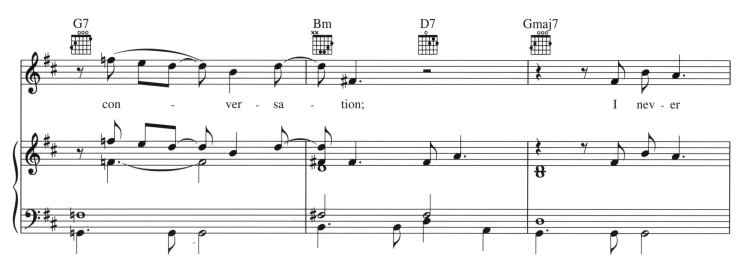

con-ver-sa-tion; I nev-er

KILLING ME SOFTLY
WITH HIS SONG

Words by NORMAN GIMBEL
Music by CHARLES FOX

Copyright © 1972 Rodali Music and Fox-Gimbel Productions, Inc.
All Rights on behalf of Rodali Music Administered by Sony/ATV Music Publishing, 8 Music Square West, Nashville, TN 37203
International Copyright Secured   All Rights Reserved

THE LADY IS A TRAMP
from BABES IN ARMS

Words by LORENZ HART
Music by RICHARD RODGERS

Moderato

I get too hun-gry for din - ner at eight,

I like the thea - tre but

nev - er come late. I nev - er

Copyright © 1937 by Williamson Music and The Estate Of Lorenz Hart in the United States
Copyright Renewed
All Rights on behalf of The Estate Of Lorenz Hart Administered by WB Music Corp.
International Copyright Secured   All Rights Reserved

Won't dish the dirt with the rest of the girls, _____

That's why the la-dy is a tramp. _____ I like the

free fresh wind in my hair, _____

Life with-out care. _____ I'm broke, ___ it's oke, ___

LET IT BE

Words and Music by JOHN LENNON
and PAUL McCARTNEY

Slowly

When I find my-self __ in times of trou-ble,
Instrumental

Moth-er Mar - y comes to me speak-ing words of wis - dom; let it

be. _____ And in my hour of dark - ness, she is

Copyright © 1970 Sony/ATV Songs LLC
Copyright Renewed
All Rights Administered by Sony/ATV Music Publishing, 8 Music Square West, Nashville, TN 37203
International Copyright Secured   All Rights Reserved

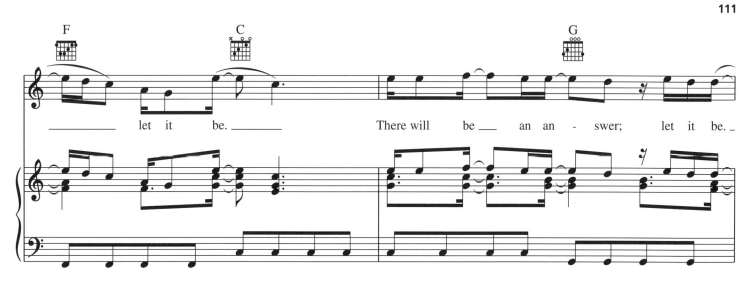

let it be. ____ There will be ___ an an-swer; let it be. ___

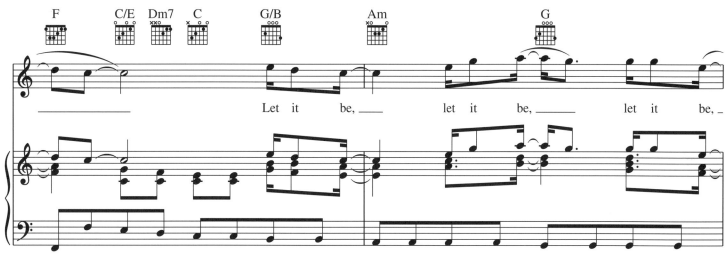

Let it be, ____ let it be, _____ let it be, __

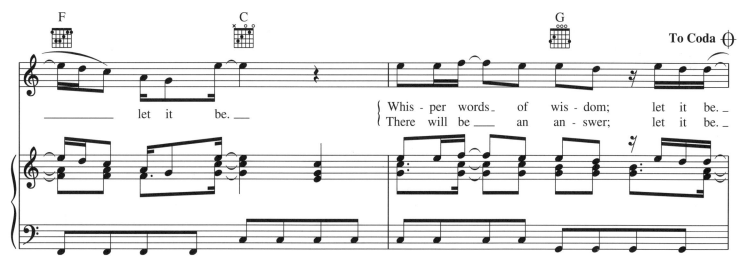

{ Whis-per words_ of wis-dom; let it be. _
{ There will be ___ an an-swer; let it be. _

To Coda ⊕

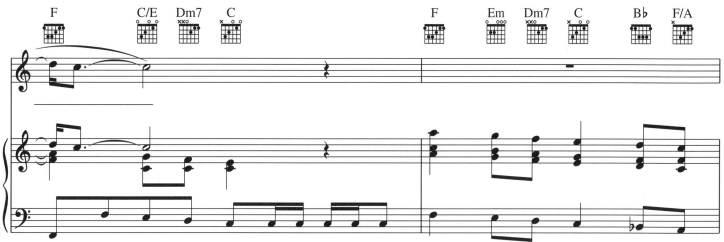

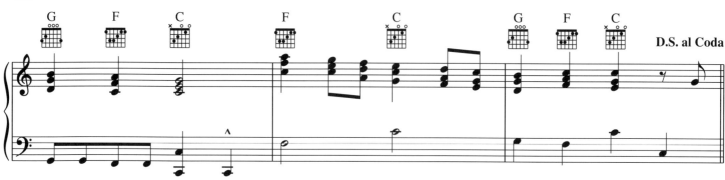

D.S. al Coda

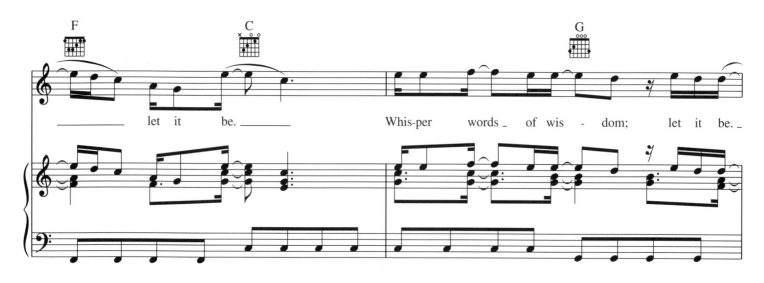

CODA

Let it be, ____ let it be, _____ let it be, _

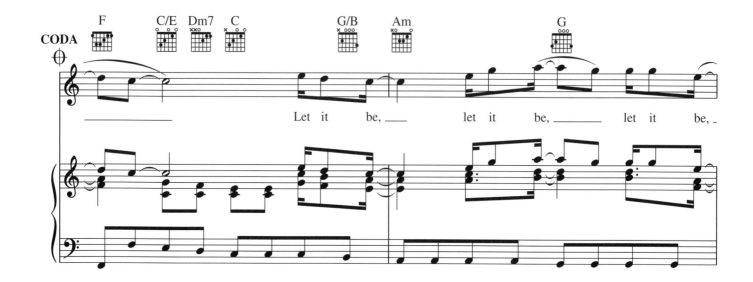

____ let it be. ____ Whis-per words_ of wis - dom; let it be. _

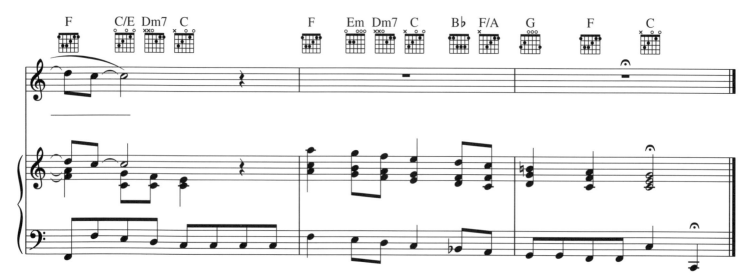

LONGER

Words and Music by
DAN FOGELBERG

Moderate Ballad

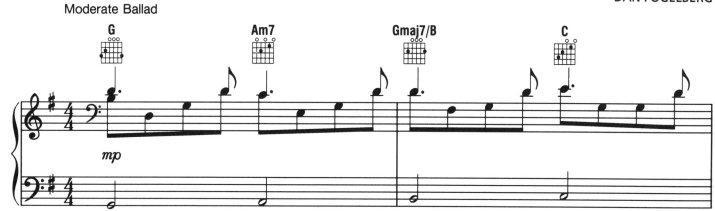

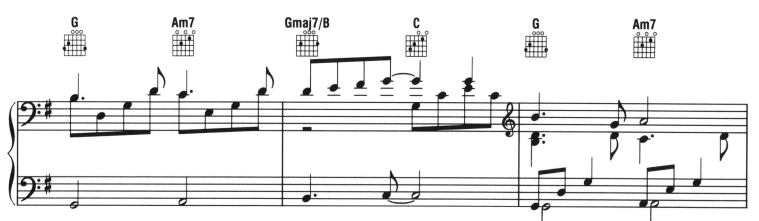

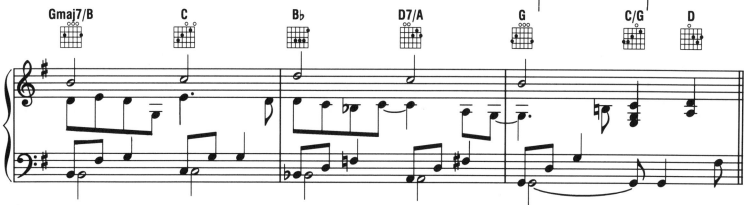

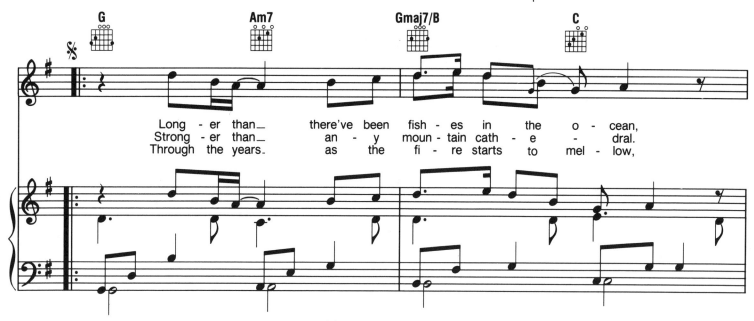

Long - er than__ there've been fish - es in the o - cean,
Strong - er than__ an - y moun - tain cath - e - dral.
Through the years__ as the fi - re starts to mel - low,

© 1979 EMI APRIL MUSIC INC. and HICKORY GROVE MUSIC
All Rights Controlled and Administered by EMI APRIL MUSIC INC.
All Rights Reserved   International Copyright Secured   Used by Permission

114

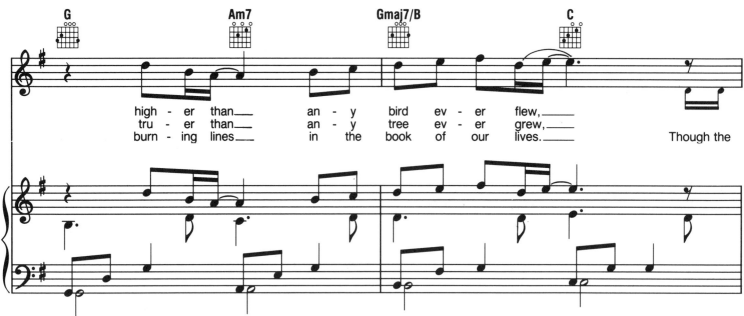

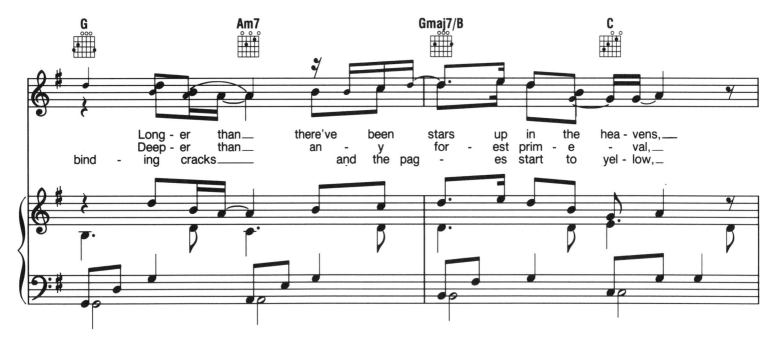

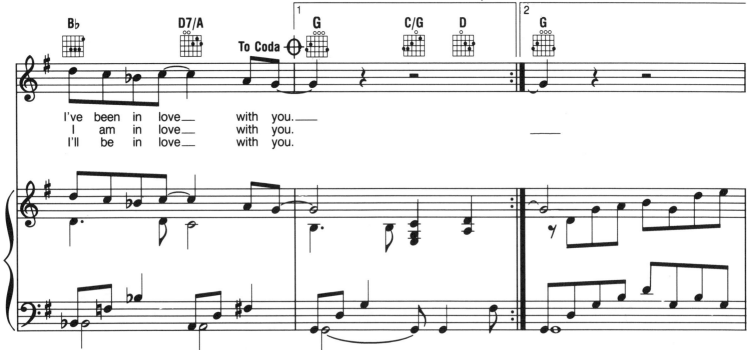

116

LOVE ME TENDER

Words and Music by ELVIS PRESLEY
and VERA MATSON

Moderately slow

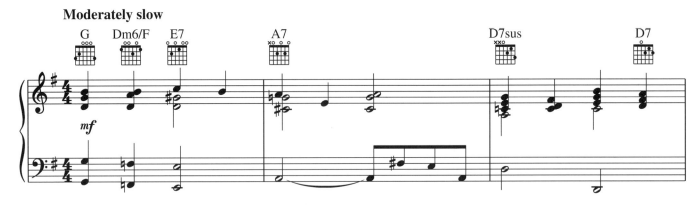

Love me ten - der, love me sweet,
Love me ten - der, love me long,
Love me ten - der, love me dear,
When at last my dreams come true,

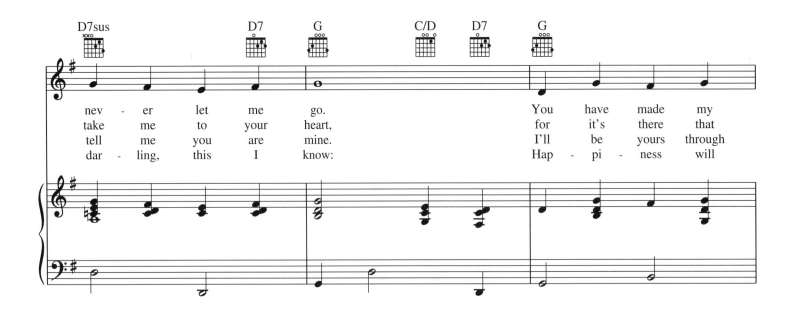

nev - er let me go.
take me to your heart,
tell me you are mine.
dar - ling, this I know:

You have made my
for it's there that
I'll be yours through
Hap - pi - ness will

Copyright © 1956 by Elvis Presley Music, Inc.
Copyright Renewed and Assigned to Elvis Presley Music (Administered by R&H Music)
International Copyright Secured   All Rights Reserved

LULLABY OF THE LEAVES

Words by JOE YOUNG
Music by BERNICE PETKERE

Moderato

Rust - ling of the leaves

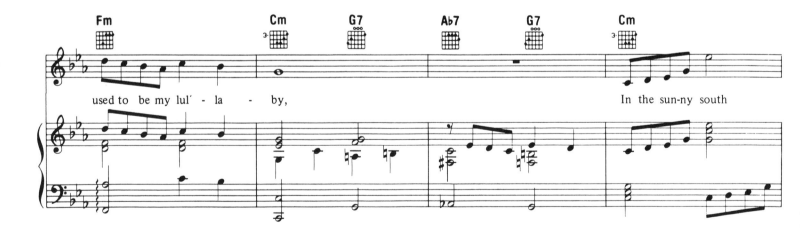

used to be my lul´ - la - by,

In the sun-ny south

© 1932 IRVING BERLIN, INC.
© Renewed WAROCK CORP. and BOURNE CO.
All Rights Reserved

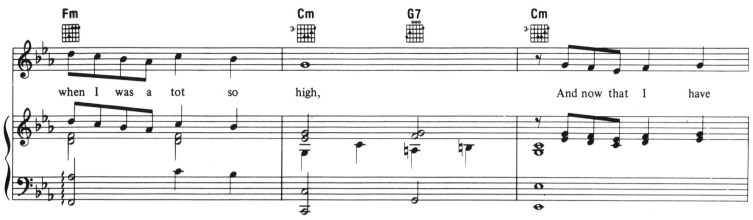

when I was a tot so high, And now that I have

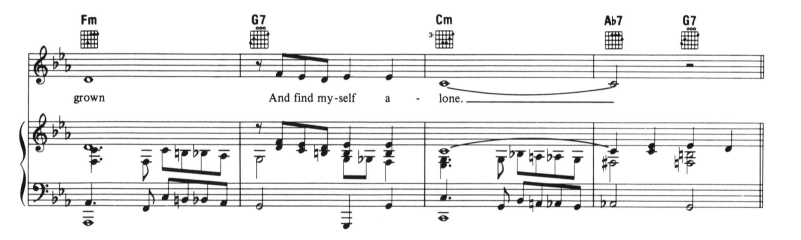

grown And find my-self a - lone.

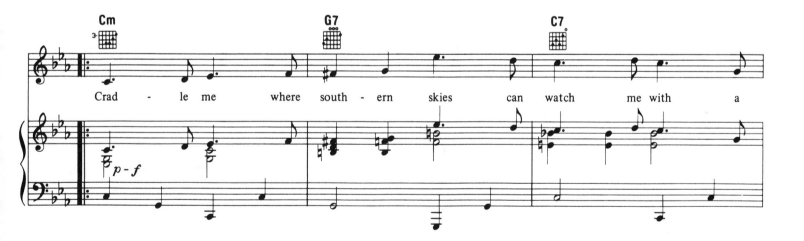

Crad - le me where south - ern skies can watch me with a

mil - lion eyes, Oh sing me to sleep, Lul - la - by Of The

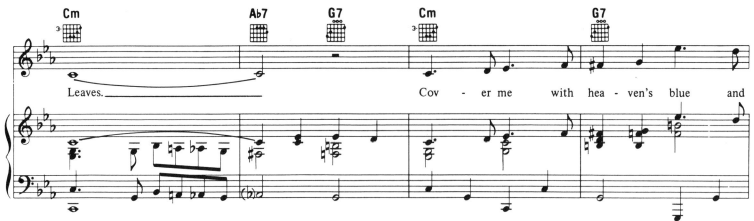

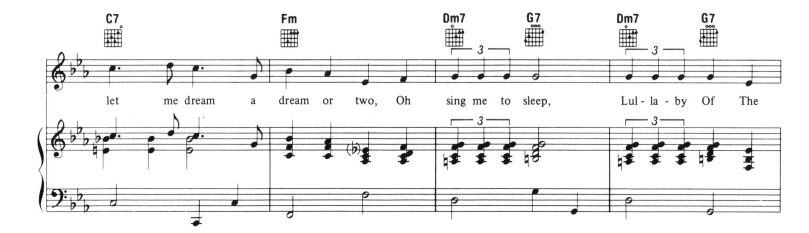

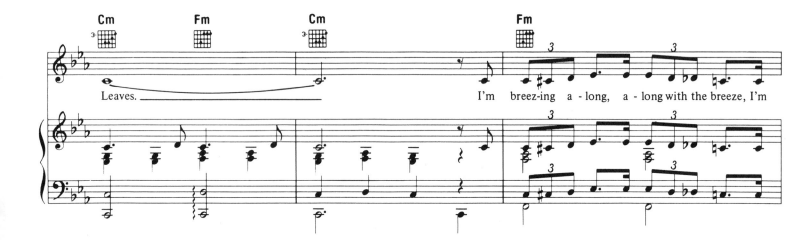

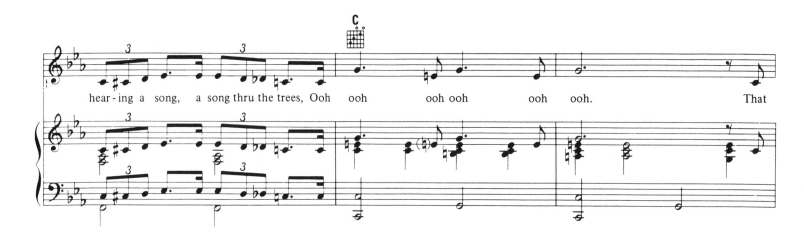

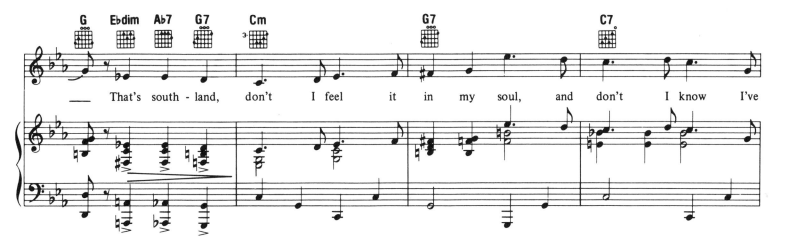

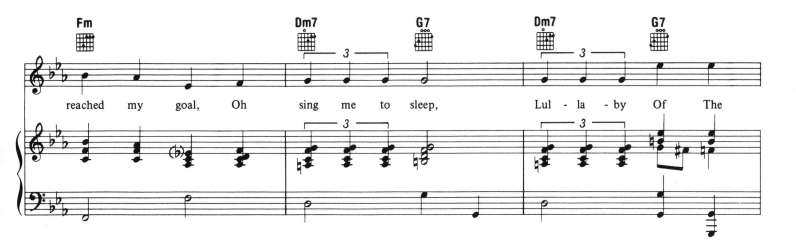

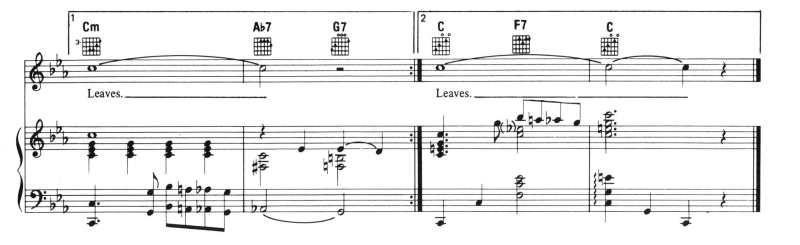

MEMORY
from CATS

Music by ANDREW LLOYD WEBBER
Text by TREVOR NUNN after T.S. ELIOT

Freely ♩. = 50

Mid - night._____ Not a sound from the pave - ment._____ Has the moon lost her
Me - mory_____ all a - lone in the moon - light_____ I can smile at the

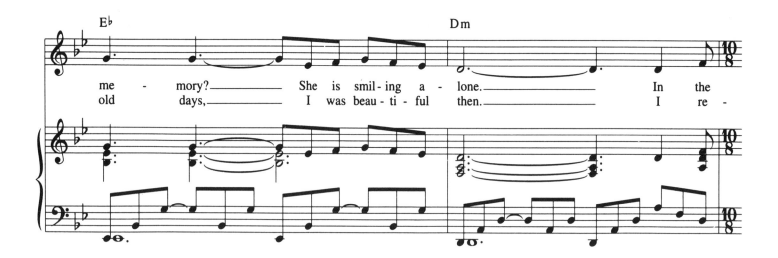

me - mory?_____ She is smil - ing a - lone._____ In the
old days,_____ I was beau - ti - ful then._____ I re -

Music Copyright © 1981 The Really Useful Group Ltd.
Text Copyright © 1981 Trevor Nunn and Set Copyrights Ltd.
All Rights for The Really Useful Group Ltd. for the United States and Canada Administered by Universal - Songs Of PolyGram International, Inc.
All Rights in the text Controlled by Faber and Faber Ltd. and Administered for the United States and Canada by R&H Music Co.
International Copyright Secured All Rights Reserved

126

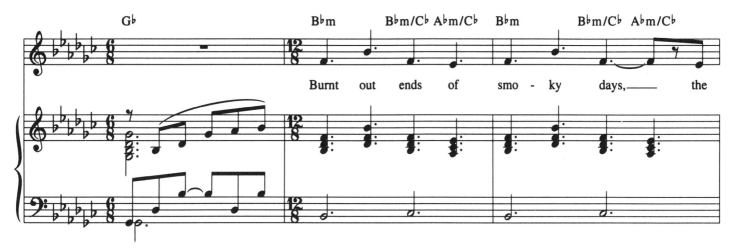

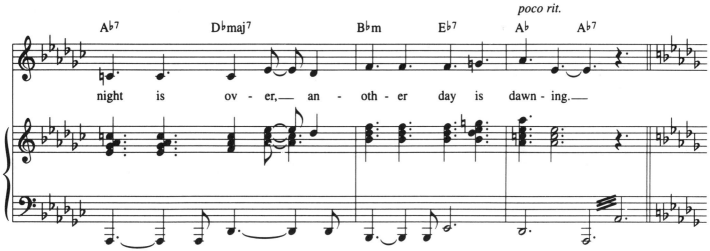

Touch me._____ It's so ea - sy to leave me_____ all a - lone with the

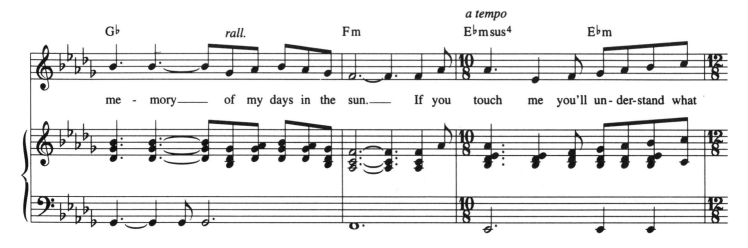

me - mory_____ of my days in the sun._____ If you touch me you'll un - der-stand what

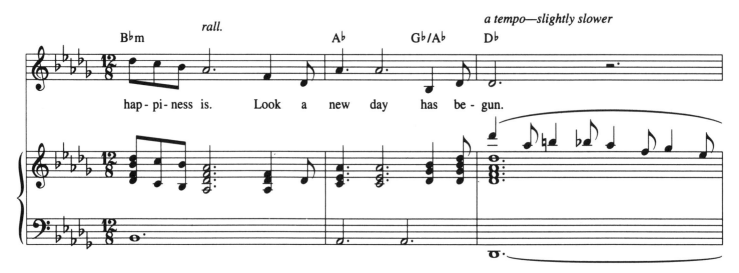

hap - pi - ness is. Look a new day has be - gun.

MONA LISA

from the Paramount Picture CAPTAIN CAREY, U.S.A.

Words and Music by JAY LIVINGSTON
and RAY EVANS

In a vil - la in a lit - tle old I - tal - ian town lives a girl whose beau - ty shames the rose. Man - y yearn to love her but their hopes all tum - ble down. What does she want? No one knows! Mo - na

Copyright © 1949 (Renewed 1976) by Famous Music Corporation.
International Copyright Secured   All Rights Reserved

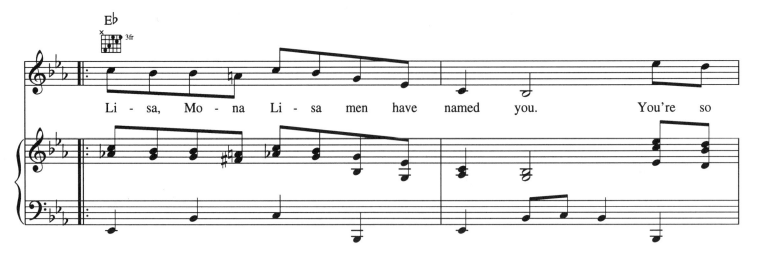

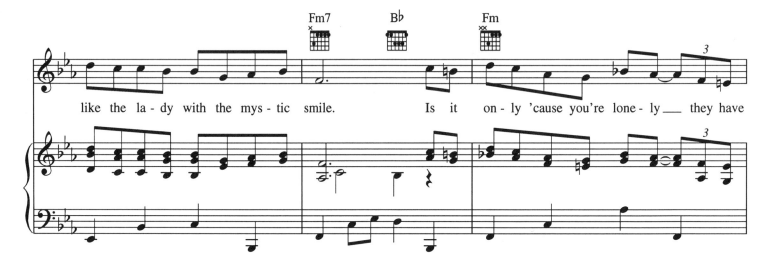

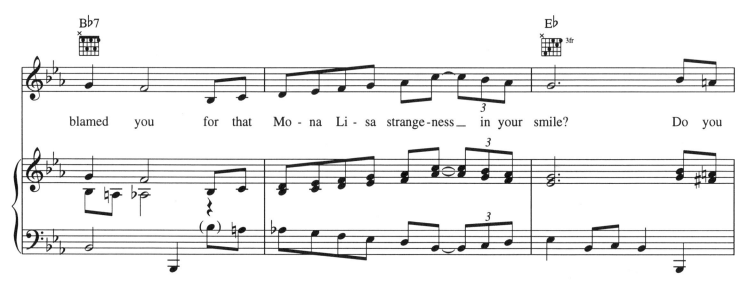

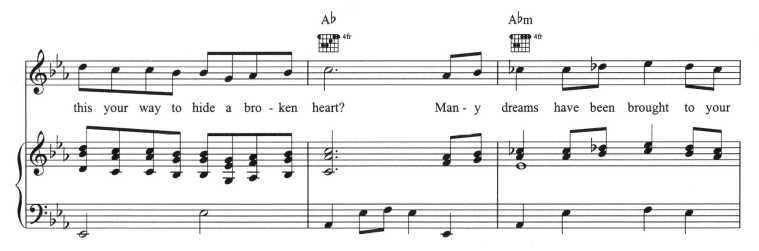

this your way to hide a bro-ken heart? Man-y dreams have been brought to your

door-step. They just lie there, and they die there. Are you

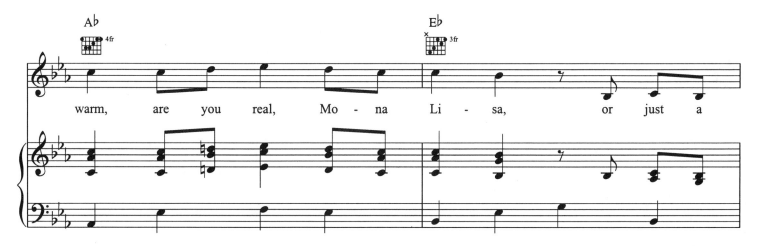

warm, are you real, Mo-na Li-sa, or just a

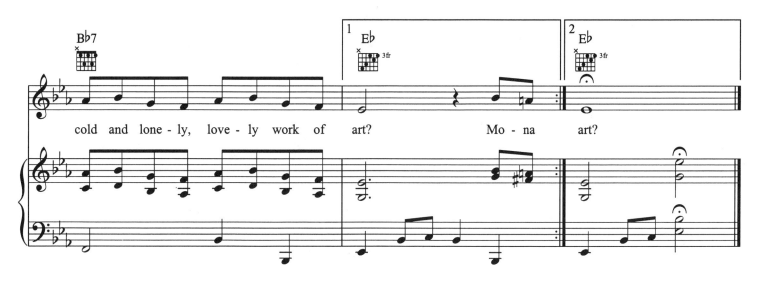

cold and lone-ly, love-ly work of art? Mo-na art?

MOOD INDIGO

from SOPHISTICATED LADIES

Words and Music by DUKE ELLINGTON,
IRVING MILLS and ALBANY BIGARD

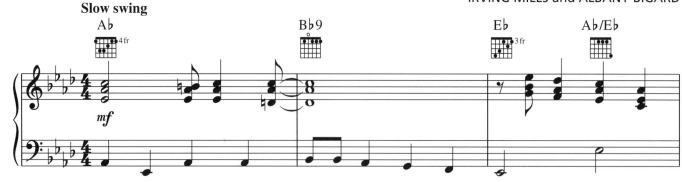

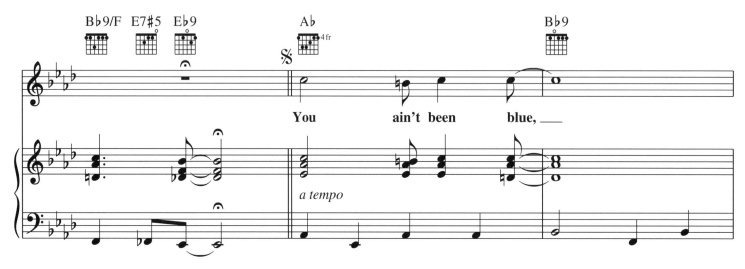

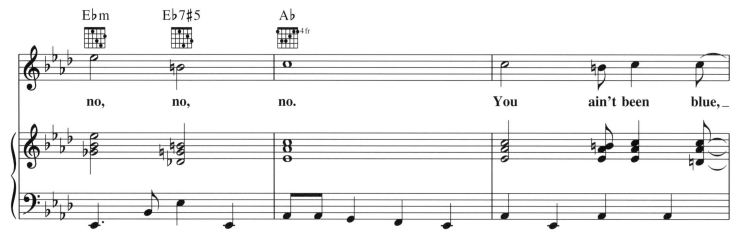

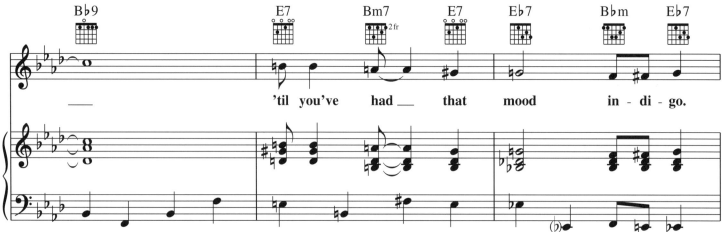

Copyright © 1931 (Renewed 1958) and Assigned to Famous Music Corporation,
EMI Mills Music Inc. and Indigo Mood Music c/o The Songwriters Guild Of America in the U.S.A
Rights for the world outside the U.S.A. Controlled by EMI Mills Music Inc. (Publishing) and Warner Bros. Publications Inc. (Print)
International Copyright Secured   All Rights Reserved

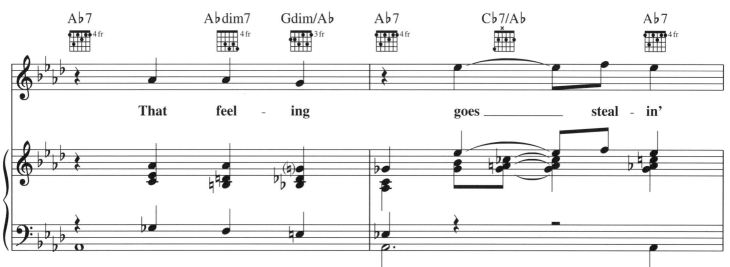

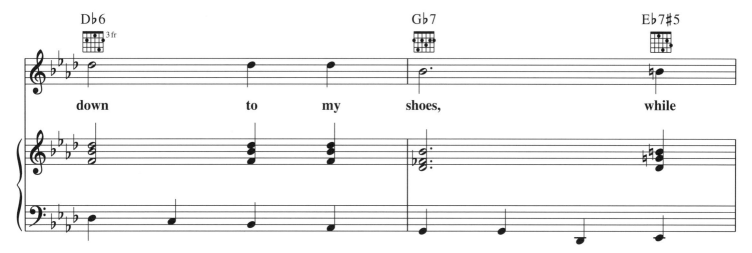

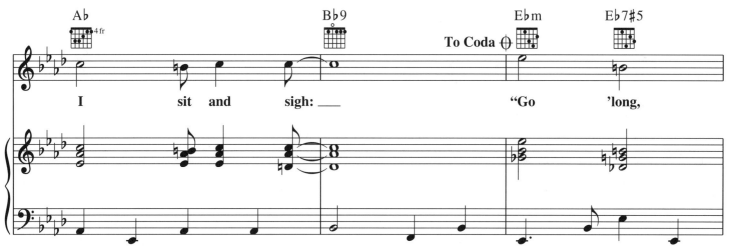

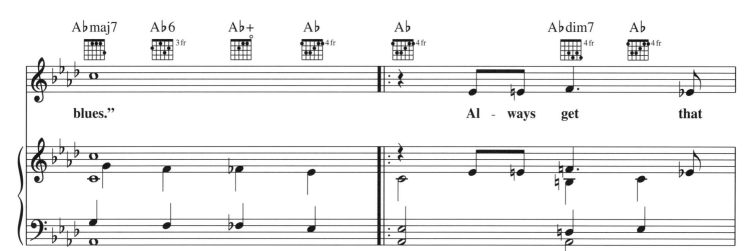

MOON RIVER

from the Paramount Picture BREAKFAST AT TIFFANY'S

Words by JOHNNY MERCER
Music by HENRY MANCINI

Copyright © 1961 (Renewed 1989) by Famous Music Corporation
International Copyright Secured   All Rights Reserved

MOONLIGHT IN VERMONT

Words and Music by JOHN BLACKBURN
and KARL SUESSDORF

Copyright © 1944 (Renewed 1972) Michael H. Goldsen, Inc. and Johnny R. Music Company in the U.S.
All Rights outside the U.S. Controlled by Michael H. Goldsen, Inc.
International Copyright Secured   All Rights Reserved

141

MOONGLOW

Words and Music by WILL HUDSON,
EDDIE DE LANGE and IRVING MILLS

Copyright © 1934 Mills Music, Inc., New York
Copyright Renewed, Assigned to Mills Music, Inc. and Scarsdale Music Corporation, New York for the United States
All Rights outside the United States Controlled by Mills Music, Inc.
International Copyright Secured   All Rights Reserved
Used by Permission

MORE
(Ti guardero' nel cuore)
from the film MONDO CANE

Music by NINO OLIVIERO and RIZ ORTOLANI
Italian Lyrics by MARCELLO CIORCIOLINI
English Lyrics by NORMAN NEWELL

Copyright © 1962 by C.A.M. S.r.l. - Rome (Italy), Via Cola di Rienzo, 152
International Copyright Secured   All Rights Reserved

MY FUNNY VALENTINE

from BABES IN ARMS

Words by LORENZ HART
Music by RICHARD RODGERS

Copyright © 1937 by Williamson Music and The Estate Of Lorenz Hart in the United States
Copyright Renewed
All Rights on behalf of The Estate Of Lorenz Hart Administered by WB Music Corp.
International Copyright Secured   All Rights Reserved

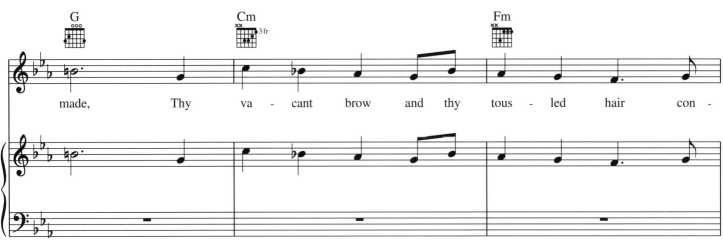

made, Thy va - cant brow and thy tous - led hair con -

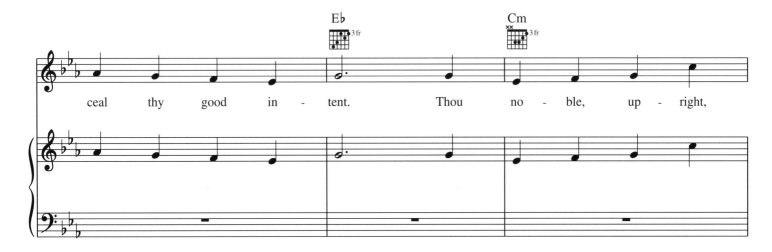

ceal thy good in - tent. Thou no - ble, up - right,

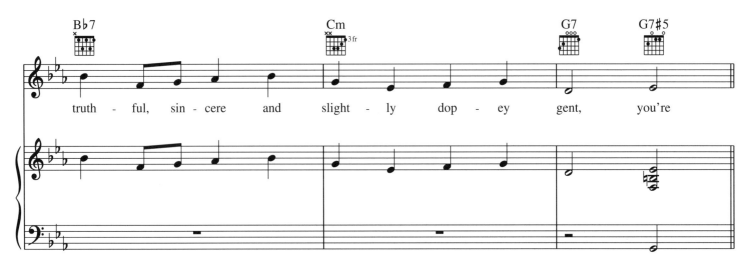

truth - ful, sin - cere and slight - ly dop - ey gent, you're

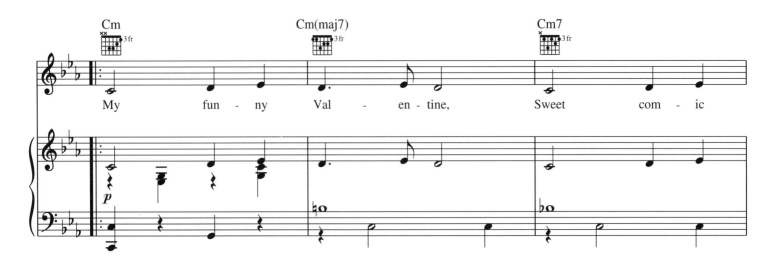

My fun - ny Val - en - tine, Sweet com - ic

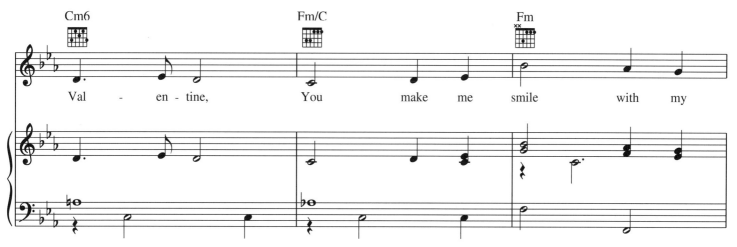

Val - en - tine, You make me smile with my

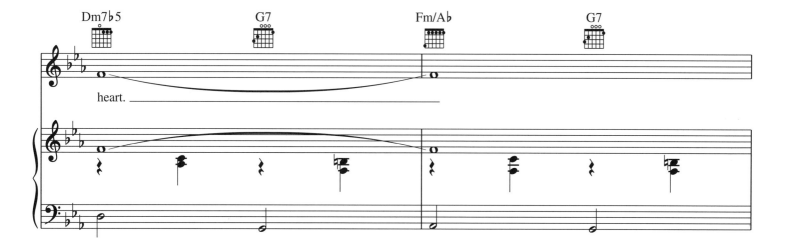

heart. _____

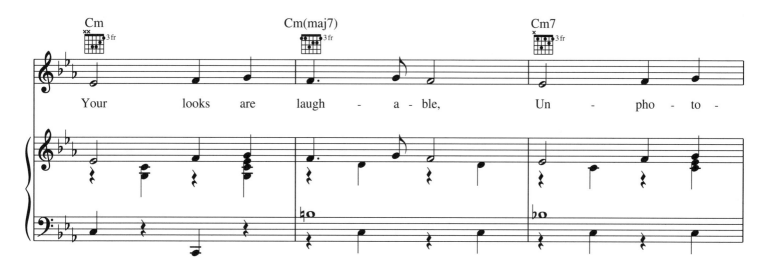

Your looks are laugh - a - ble, Un - pho - to -

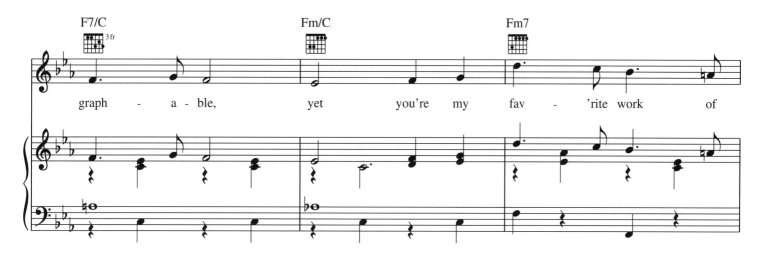

graph - a - ble, yet you're my fav - 'rite work of

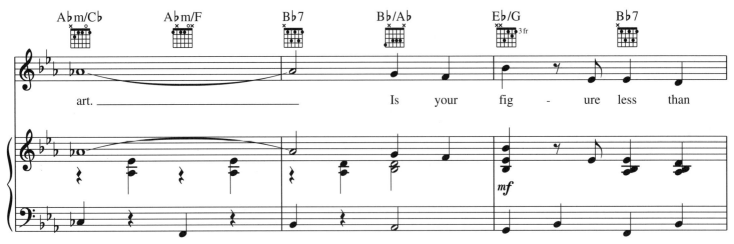

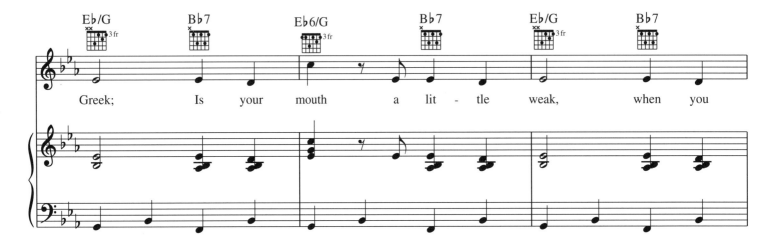

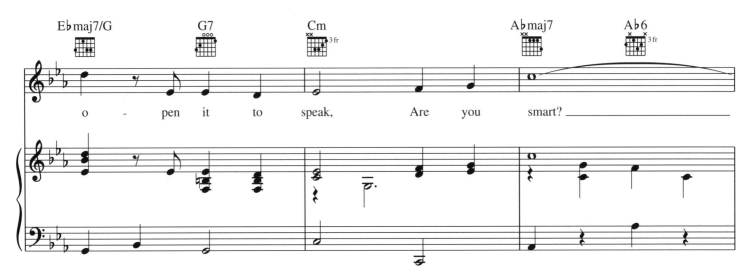

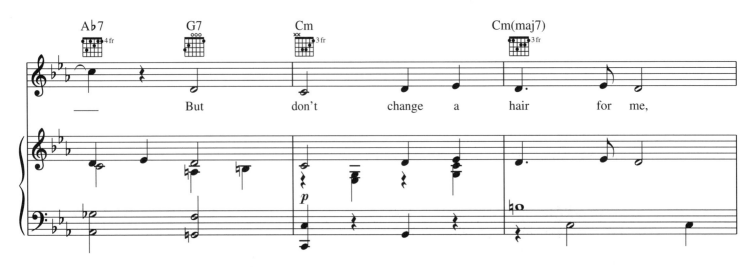

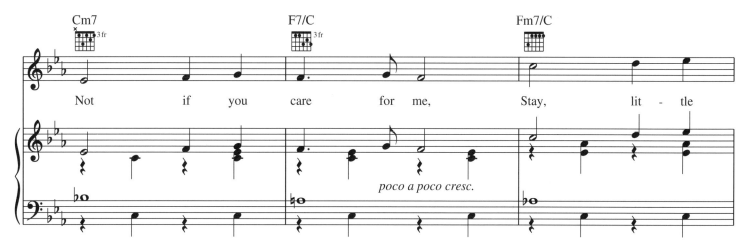

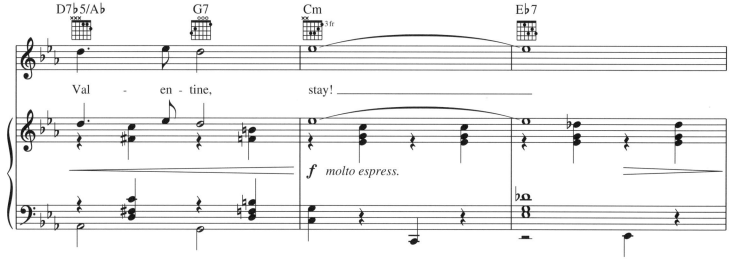

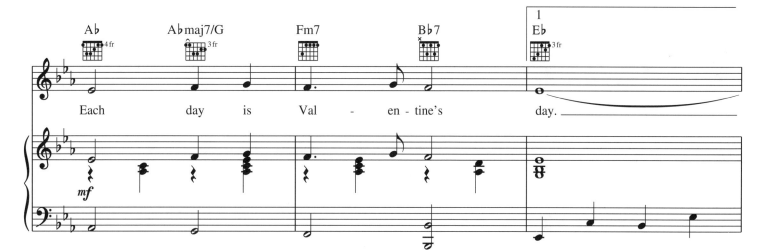

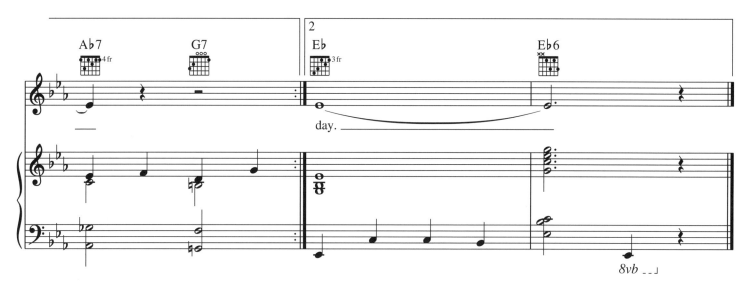

MY FAVORITE THINGS
from THE SOUND OF MUSIC

Lyrics by OSCAR HAMMERSTEIN II
Music by RICHARD RODGERS

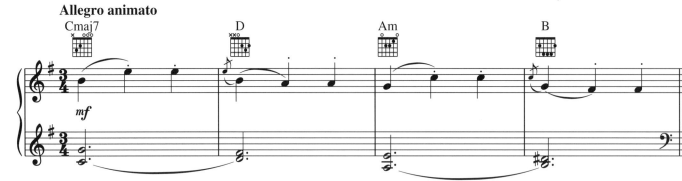

Rain - drops on ros - es and whis - kers on kit - tens, Bright cop - per

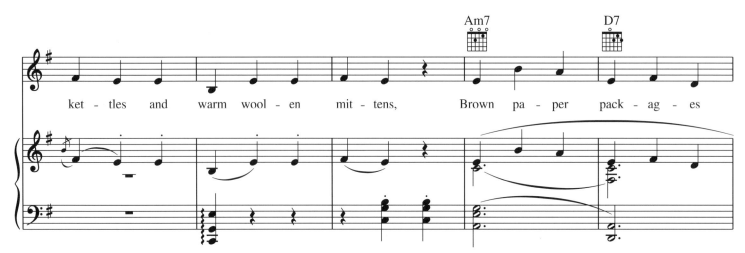

ket - tles and warm wool - en mit - tens, Brown pa - per pack - ag - es

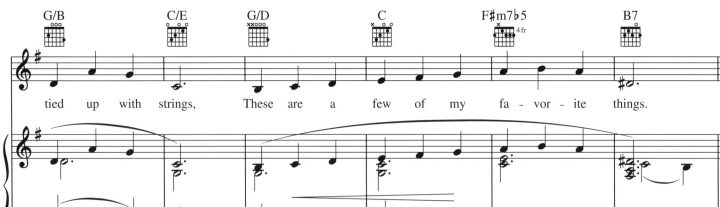

tied up with strings, These are a few of my fa - vor - ite things.

Copyright © 1959 by Richard Rodgers and Oscar Hammerstein II
Copyright Renewed
WILLIAMSON MUSIC owner of publication and allied rights throughout the world
International Copyright Secured   All Rights Reserved

ON THE STREET WHERE YOU LIVE

from MY FAIR LADY

Words by ALAN JAY LERNER
Music by FREDERICK LOEWE

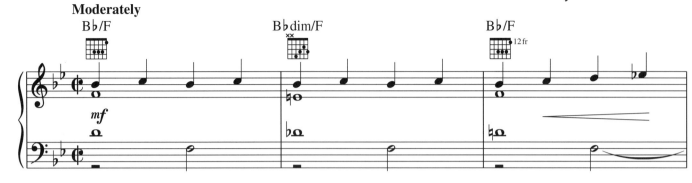

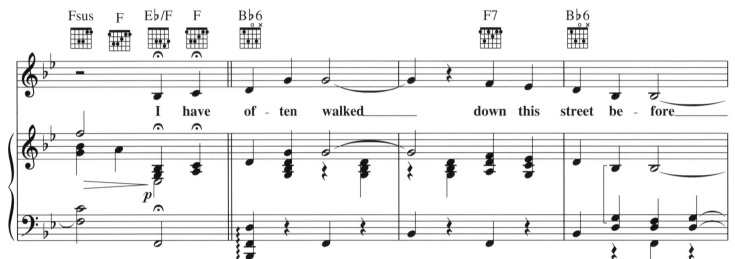

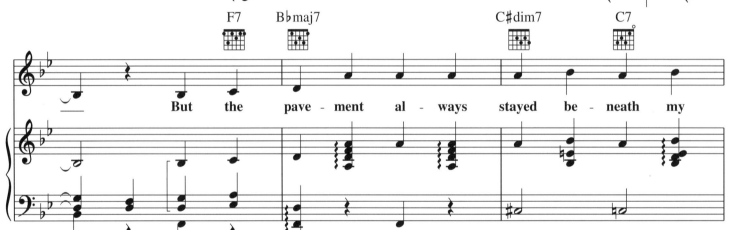

Copyright © 1956 by Alan Jay Lerner and Frederick Loewe
Copyright Renewed
Chappell & Co. owner of publication and allied rights throughout the world
International Copyright Secured   All Rights Reserved

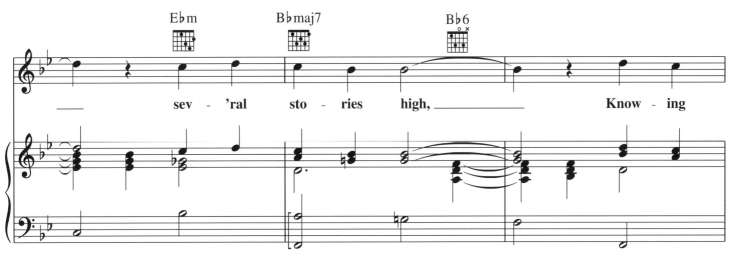

sev - 'ral sto - ries high, _____ Know - ing

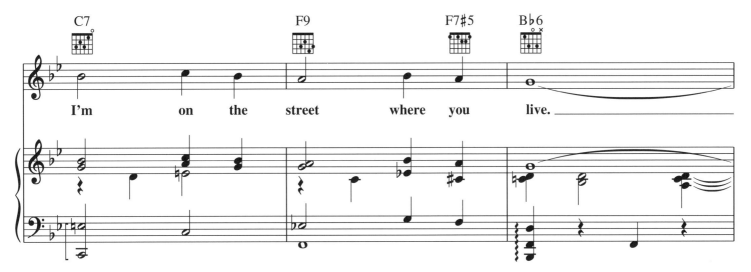

I'm on the street where you live. _____

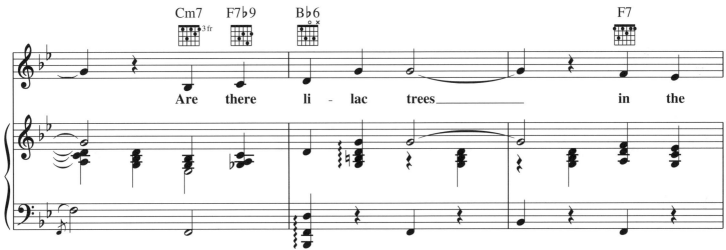

Are there li - lac trees_____ in the

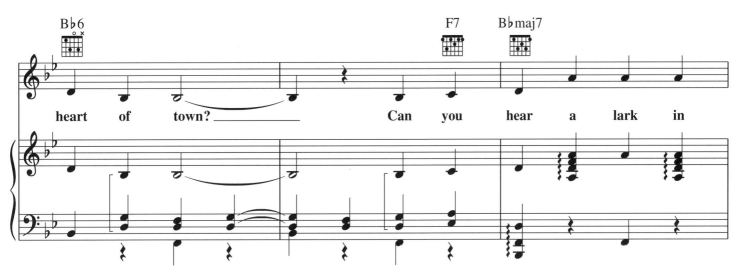

heart of town? _____ Can you hear a lark in

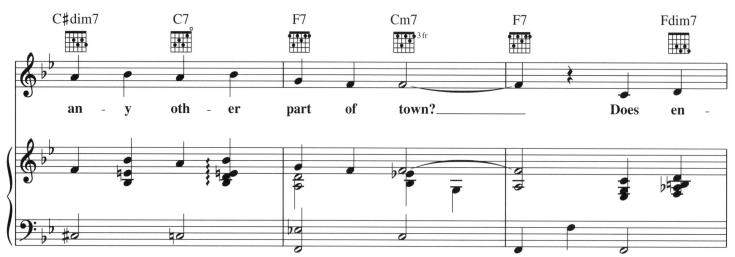

an - y oth - er part of town?_____ Does en -

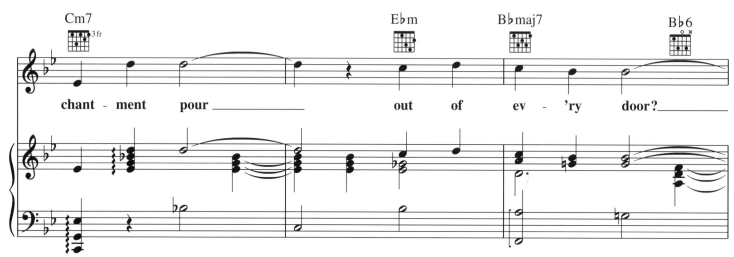

chant - ment pour _____ out of ev - 'ry door?_____

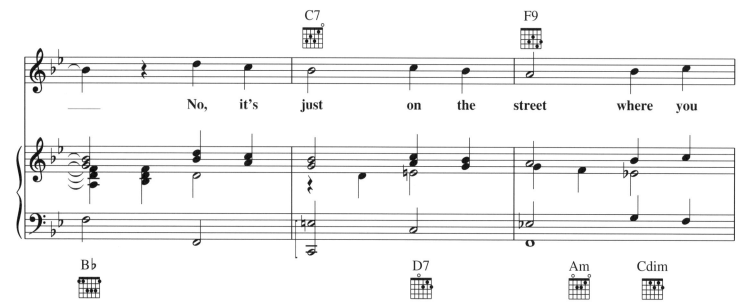

No, it's just on the street where you

live._____ And oh,_____ the tow - er - ing

PIANO MAN

Words and Music by
BILLY JOEL

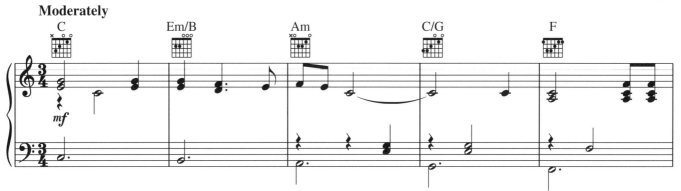

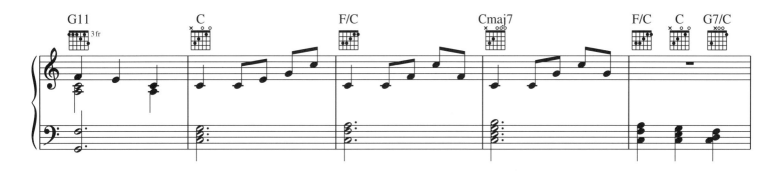

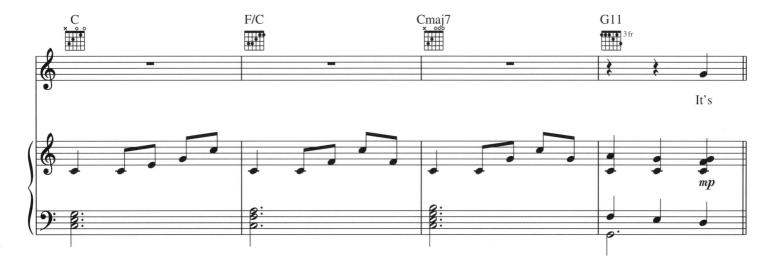

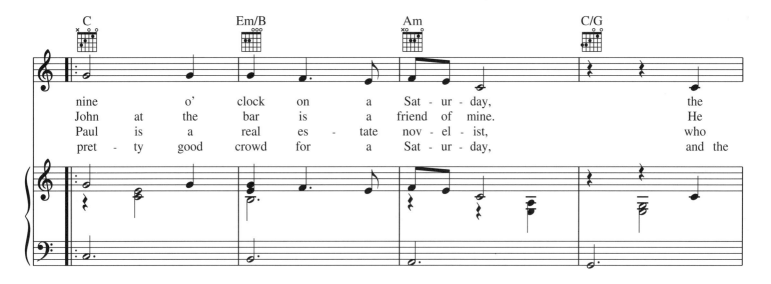

nine   o'   clock   on   a   Sat - ur - day,   the
John   at   the   bar   is   a   friend   of   mine.   He
Paul   is   a   real   es - tate   nov - el - ist,   who
pret - ty   good   crowd   for   a   Sat - ur - day,   and the

© 1973, 1974 JOEL SONGS
All Rights Reserved   International Copyright Secured   Used by Permission

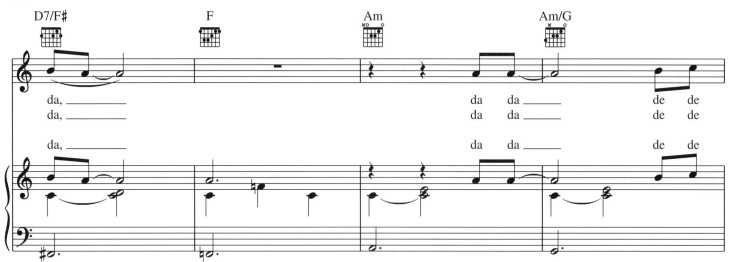

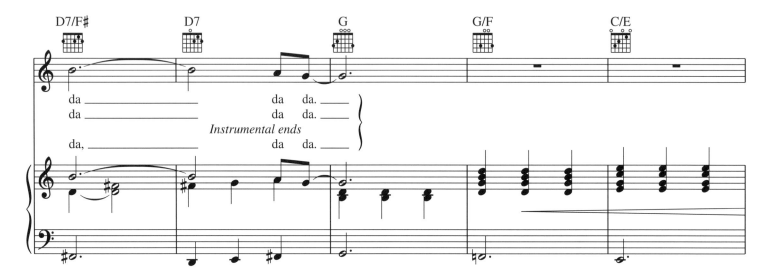

Instrumental ends

Sing us a song, you're the pia - no man. _____

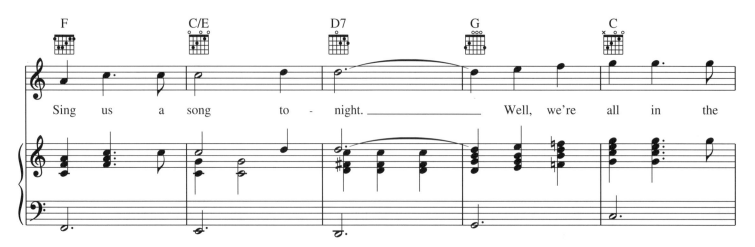

Sing us a song to - night. _____ Well, we're all in the

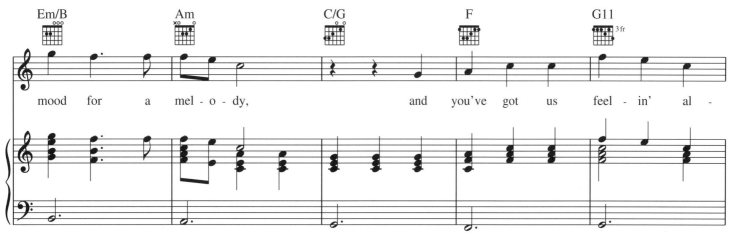

mood for a mel - o - dy, and you've got us feel - in' al -

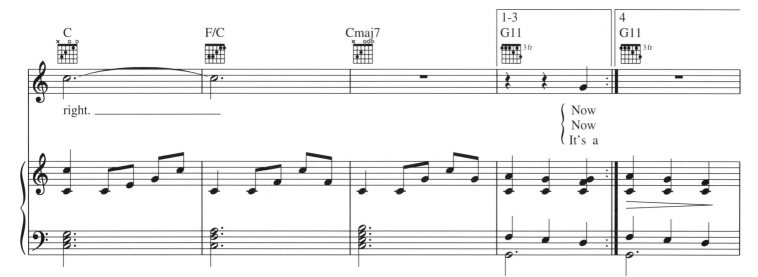

right. _____

Now
Now
It's a

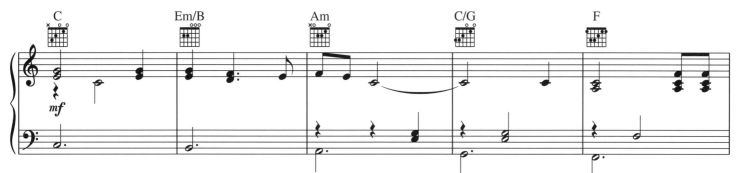

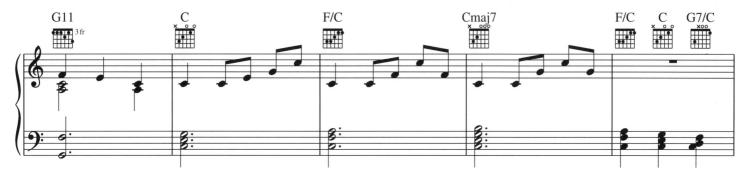

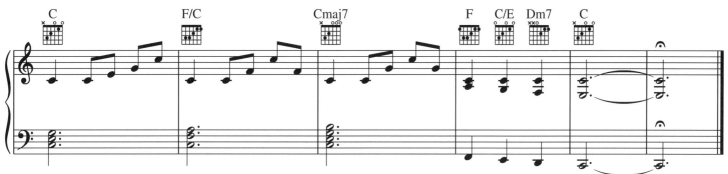

PEOPLE
from FUNNY GIRL

Words by BOB MERRILL
Music by JULE STYNE

Copyright © 1963, 1964 by Bob Merrill and Jule Styne
Copyright Renewed
All Rights Administered by Chappell & Co.
International Copyright Secured   All Rights Reserved

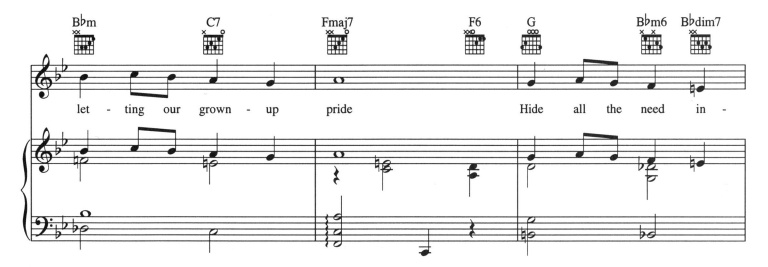

need - ing oth - er chil - dren,_____ and yet,

Bbm C7 Fmaj7 F6 G Bbm6 Bbdim7

let - ting our grown - up pride Hide all the need in -

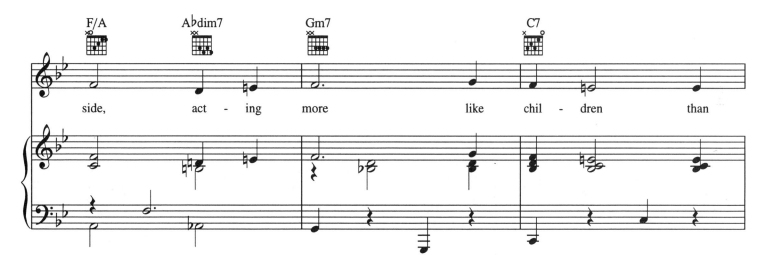

F/A Abdim7 Gm7 C7

side, act - ing more like chil - dren than

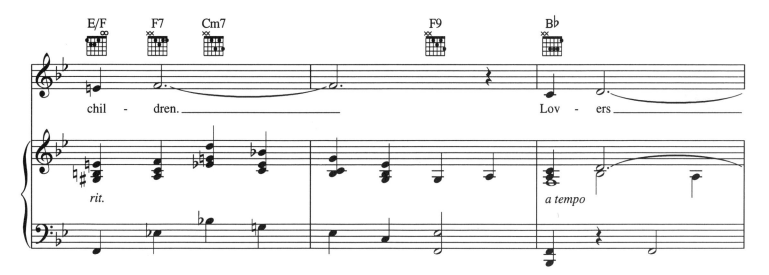

E/F F7 Cm7 F9 Bb

chil - dren._____ Lov - ers_____

rit.   *a tempo*

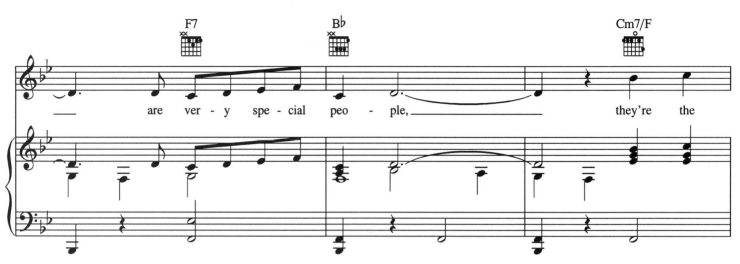

are ver-y spe-cial peo-ple,_____ they're the

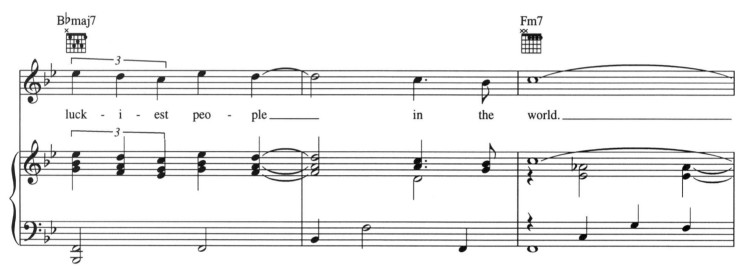

luck-i-est peo-ple _____ in the world._____

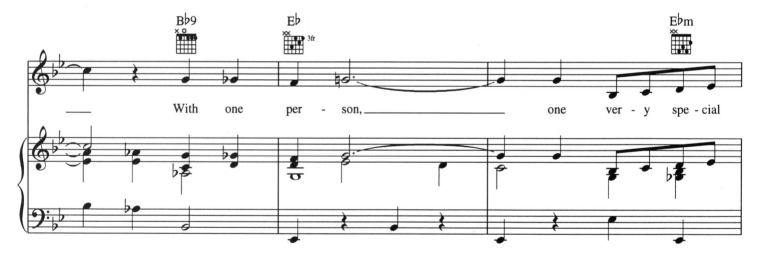

With one per-son,_____ one ver-y spe-cial

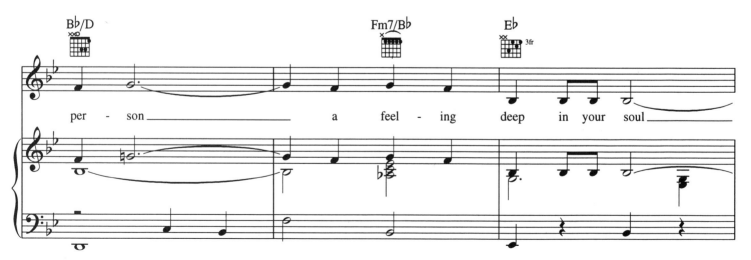

per-son _____ a feel-ing deep in your soul _____

THE RAINBOW CONNECTION

from THE MUPPET MOVIE

Words and Music by PAUL WILLIAMS
and KENNETH L. ASCHER

Moderately, with a lilt

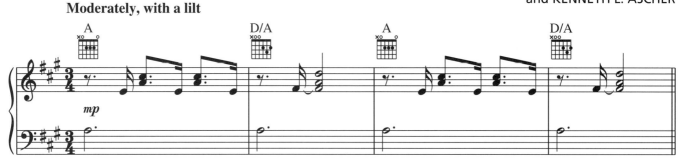

Why are there so man-y songs a-bout rain-bows, and
Who said that ev-'ry wish would be heard and an-swered when

what's on the oth - er side?
wished on the morn - ing star?

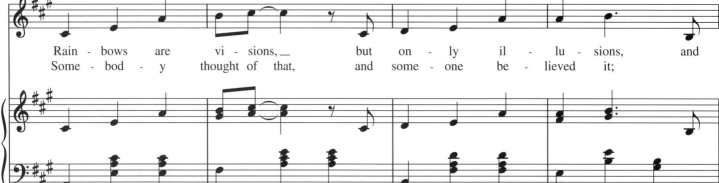

Rain - bows are vi - sions,__ but on - ly il - lu - sions, and
Some - bod - y thought of that, and some - one be - lieved it;

Copyright © 1979 Jim Henson Productions, Inc.
All Rights Administered by Sony/ATV Music Publishing, 8 Music Square West, Nashville, TN 37203
International Copyright Secured   All Rights Reserved

lov - ers, ___ the dream - ers, ___ and me.
lov - ers, ___ the dream - ers, ___ and

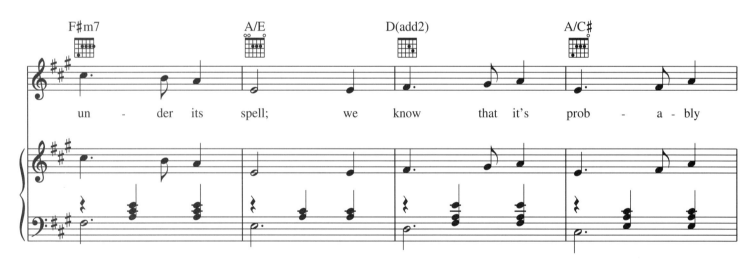

me. All of us

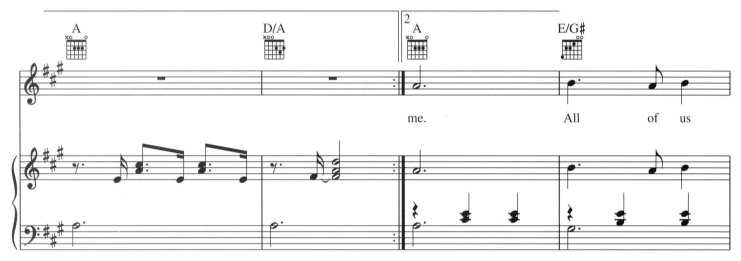

un - der its spell; we know that it's prob - a - bly

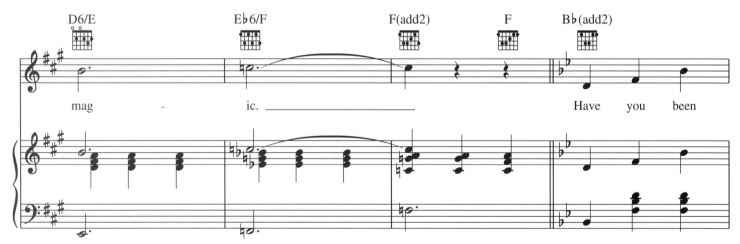

mag - ic. _____ Have you been

175

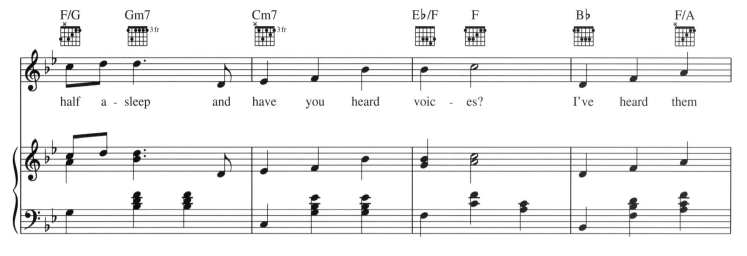

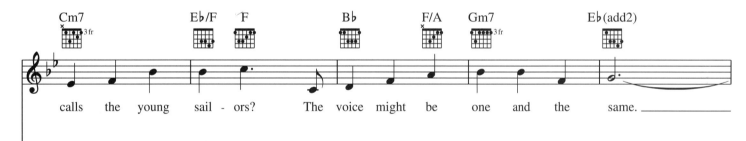

SATIN DOLL
from SOPHISTICATED LADIES

Words by JOHNNY MERCER and BILLY STRAYHORN
Music by DUKE ELLINGTON

Copyright © 1958 (Renewed 1986) and Assigned to Famous Music Corporation, WB Music Corp. and Tempo Music, Inc. c/o Music Sales Corporation in the U.S.A.
Rights for the world outside the U.S.A. Controlled by Tempo Music, Inc. c/o Music Sales Corporation
International Copyright Secured   All Rights Reserved

SAVE THE BEST FOR LAST

Words and Music by PHIL GALDSTON,
JON LIND and WENDY WALDMAN

© 1989 EMI VIRGIN SONGS, INC., BIG MYSTIQUE MUSIC, UNIVERSAL - POLYGRAM INTERNATIONAL PUBLISHING, INC., EMI LONGITUDE MUSIC,
MOON AND STARS MUSIC and KAZZOOM MUSIC INC.
All Rights for BIG MYSTIQUE MUSIC Controlled and Administered by EMI VIRGIN SONGS, INC.
All Rights for MOON AND STARS MUSIC Controlled and Administered by EMI LONGITUDE MUSIC
All Rights Reserved   International Copyright Secured   Used by Permission

It's not the way ___ I hoped ___ or ___ how ___
Some - times the ver - y thing ___ you're ___ look -

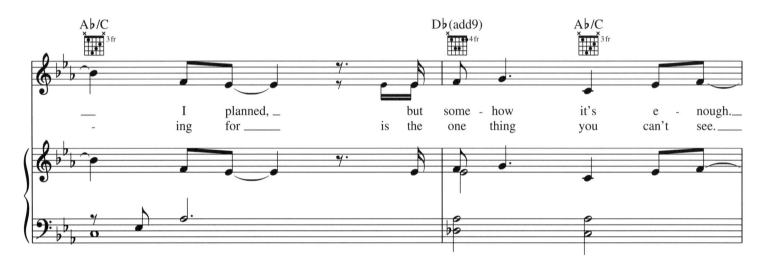

___ I planned, ___ but some - how it's e - nough. ___
- ing for ___ is the one thing you can't see. ___

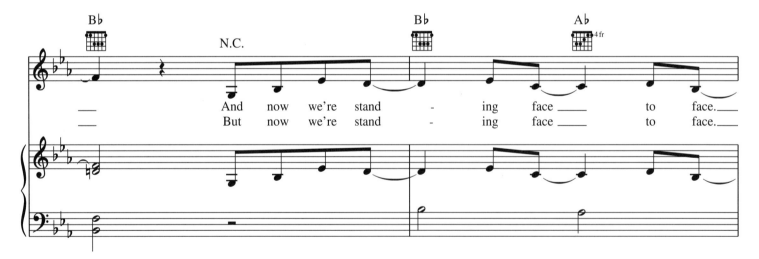

And now we're stand - ing face ___ to face. ___
But now we're stand - ing face ___ to face. ___

Is - n't this world ___ a cra - zy place? ___

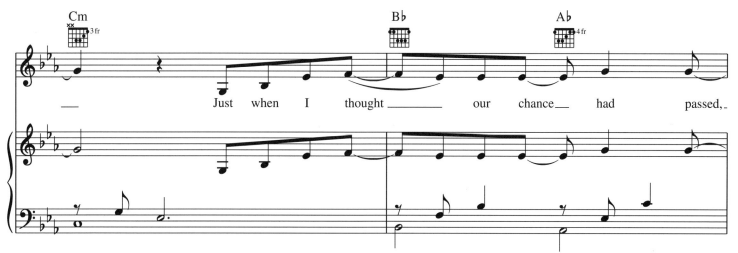

Just when I thought _____ our chance __ had passed, _

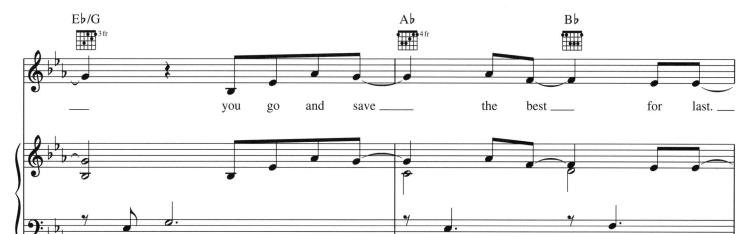

_ you go and save _____ the best ___ for last. __

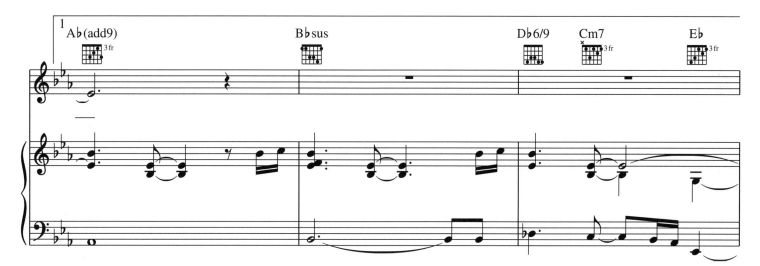

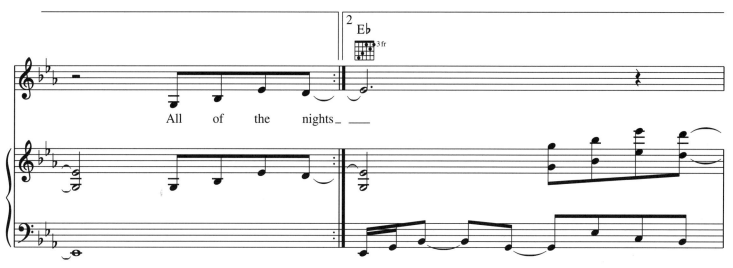

All of the nights ___

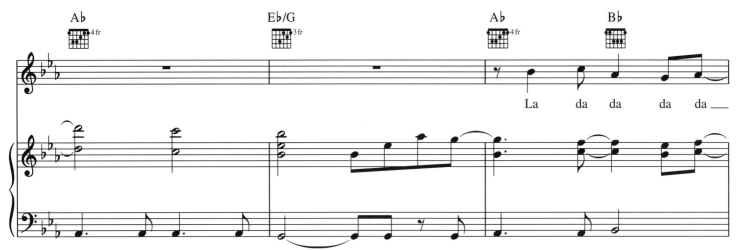

La da da da da

da da.

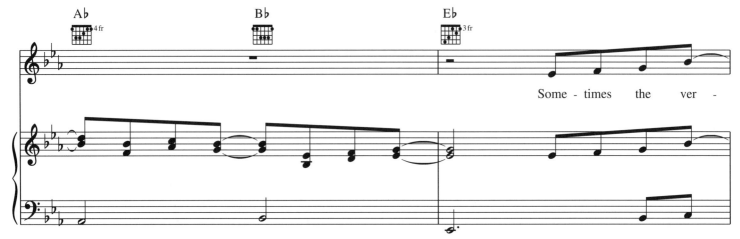

Some - times the ver -

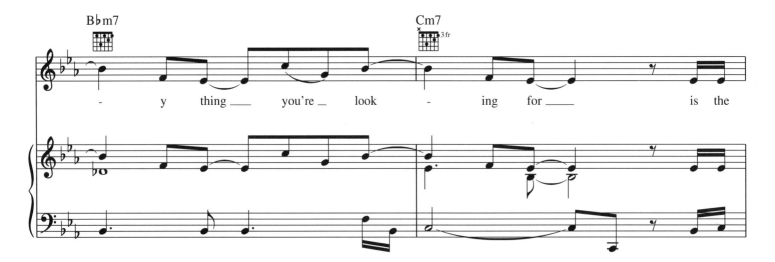

- y thing you're look - ing for is the

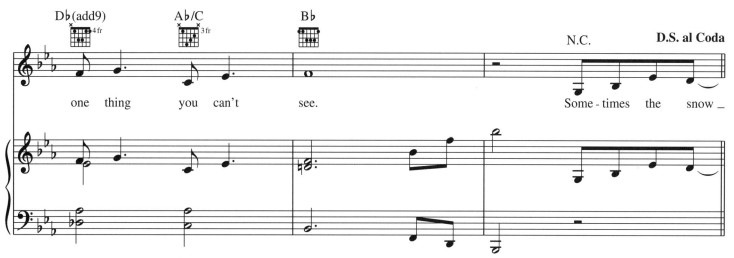

one thing you can't see. Some-times the snow

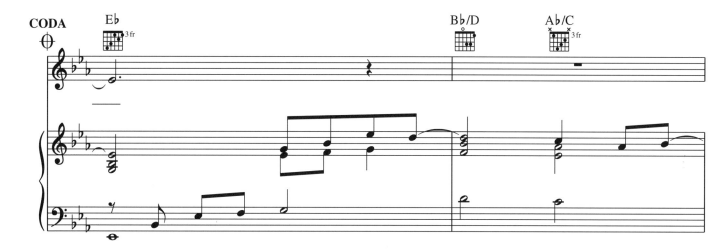

You went and saved the best for last.

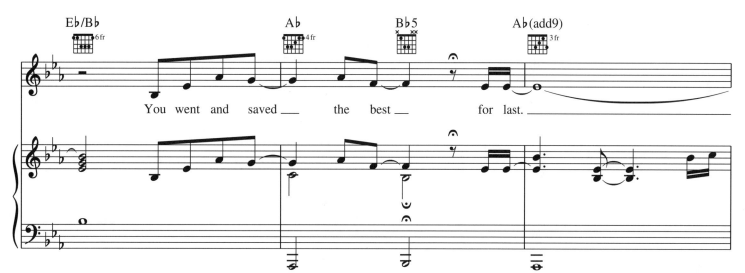

Yeah.

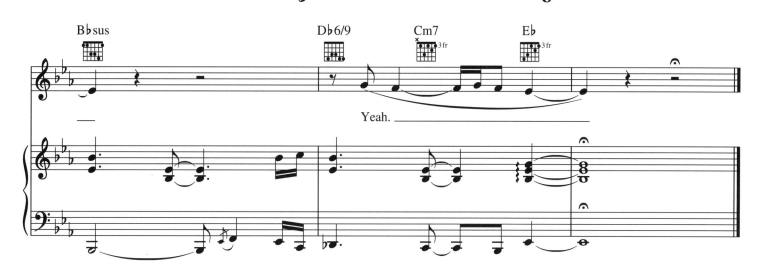

SEPTEMBER SONG
from the Musical Play KNICKERBOCKER HOLIDAY

Words by MAXWELL ANDERSON
Music by KURT WEILL

TRO - © Copyright 1938 (Renewed) Hampshire House Publishing Corp., New York and Chappell & Co., Los Angeles, CA
International Copyright Secured
All Rights Reserved Including Public Performance For Profit
Used by Permission

SOME DAY MY PRINCE WILL COME

from Walt Disney's SNOW WHITE AND THE SEVEN DWARFS

Words by LARRY MOREY
Music by FRANK CHURCHILL

Rather fast

Some Day My Prince Will Come, Some
Some Day I'll find my love, Some

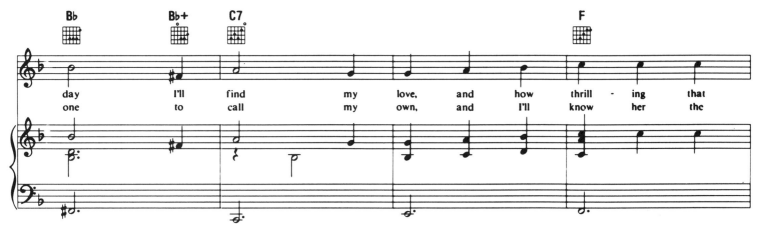

day I'll find my love, and how thrill - ing that
one to call my own, and I'll know her the

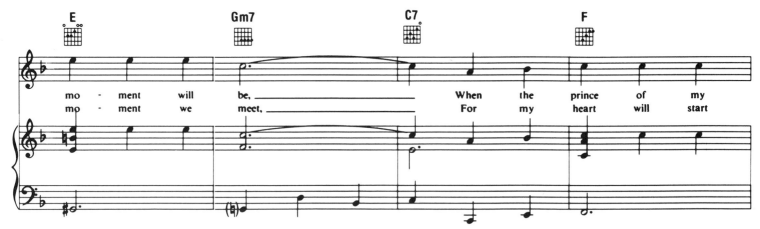

mo - ment will be, _____ When the prince of my
mo - ment we meet, _____ For my heart will start

Copyright © 1937 by Bourne Co.
Copyright Renewed
International Copyright Secured   All Rights Reserved

THE SOUND OF MUSIC
from THE SOUND OF MUSIC

Lyrics by OSCAR HAMMERSTEIN II
Music by RICHARD RODGERS

Molto moderato (tenderly)

My day in the hills has come to an end, I know. A star has come out to tell me it's time to go. But deep in the dark green shad-ows are

Copyright © 1959 by Richard Rodgers and Oscar Hammerstein II
Copyright Renewed
WILLIAMSON MUSIC owner of publication and allied rights throughout the world
International Copyright Secured   All Rights Reserved

know I will hear   what I've heard be - fore. _____

_____ My heart will be blessed   with the sound of

mf più espressivo

mu - sic _____ And I'll sing   once

dim.

more. _____   The   more. _____

p   mp

SPANISH EYES

Words by CHARLES SINGLETON and EDDIE SNYDER
Music by BERT KAEMPFERT

© 1965, 1966 (Renewed 1993, 1994) EDITION DOMA BERT KAEMPFERT
All Rights for the world, excluding Germany, Austria and Switzerland, Controlled and Administered by SCREEN GEMS-EMI MUSIC INC.
All Rights Reserved   International Copyright Secured   Used by Permission

SPEAK SOFTLY, LOVE
(Love Theme)
from the Paramount Picture THE GODFATHER

Words by LARRY KUSIK
Music by NINO ROTA

Copyright © 1972 (Renewed 2000) by Famous Music Corporation
International Copyright Secured   All Rights Reserved

STARDUST

Words by MITCHELL PARISH
Music by HOAGY CARMICHAEL

Moderately

...And now the pur - ple dusk of twi - light time

steals a - cross the mead - ows of my heart.

High up in the sky the

lit - tle stars climb, al - ways re - mind - ing me that

Copyright © 1928, 1929 by Songs Of Peer, Ltd. and EMI Mills Music, Inc.
Copyright Renewed
All Rights outside the USA Controlled by EMI Mills Music, Inc. (Publishing) and Warner Bros. Publications U.S. Inc. (Print)
International Copyright Secured   All Rights Reserved

TEARS IN HEAVEN

Words and Music by ERIC CLAPTON
and WILL JENNINGS

Would you know   my   name _____
Would you hold   my   hand _____
Would you know   my   name _____

if I   saw   you   in   heav - en?
if I   saw   you   in   heav - en?
if I   saw   you   in   heav - en?

Would   it   be   the   same _____
Would you help   me   stand _____
Would you be   the   same _____

Copyright © 1992 by E.C. Music Ltd. and Blue Sky Rider Songs
All Rights for E.C. Music Ltd. Administered by Unichappell Music Inc.
All Rights for Blue Sky Rider Songs Administered by Irving Music, Inc.
International Copyright Secured   All Rights Reserved

210

Be-yond the door ___ there's peace, I'm sure, _

STORMY WEATHER
(Keeps Rainin' All the Time)
from COTTON CLUB PARADE OF 1933

Lyric by TED KOEHLER
Music by HAROLD ARLEN

© 1933 (Renewed 1961) TED KOEHLER MUSIC and S.A. MUSIC CO.
All Rights for TED KOEHLER MUSIC Administered by FRED AHLERT MUSIC CORPORATION
All Rights Reserved

just can't get my poor ___ self to-geth-er, _____ I'm wea-ry all ___ the time, _____ the

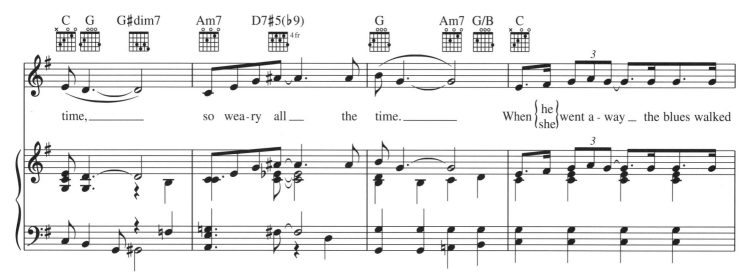

time, _____ so wea-ry all ___ the time. _____ When {he she} went a-way ___ the blues walked

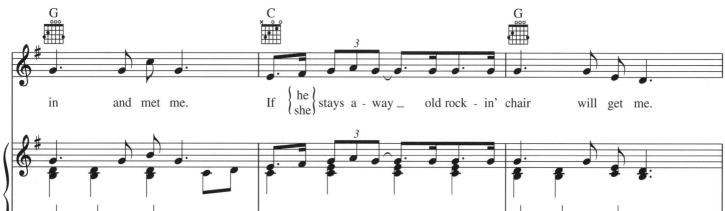

in and met me. If {he she} stays a-way ___ old rock-in' chair will get me.

All I do is pray ___ the Lord a-bove will let me walk in the sun once

A STRING OF PEARLS

from THE GLENN MILLER STORY

Words by EDDIE DE LANGE
Music by JERRY GRAY

Copyright © 1941, 1942 by Mutual Music Society, Inc.
Copyright Renewed, Assigned to Chappell & Co. and Scarsdale Music Corp.
International Copyright Secured   All Rights Reserved

THREE COINS IN THE FOUNTAIN

Words by SAMMY CAHN
Music by JULE STYNE

Three coins in the foun - tain, each one seek - ing hap - pi -

ness, thrown by three hope - ful lov - ers, which one will the foun - tain

bless? Three hearts in the foun - tain,

Copyright © 1954 by Producers Music Publishing Co. and Cahn Music Co.
Copyright Renewed
All Rights for Producers Music Publishing Co. Administered by Chappell & Co.
All Rights for Cahn Music Co. Administered by WB Music Corp.
International Copyright Secured   All Rights Reserved

A TIME FOR US
(Love Theme)
from the Paramount Picture ROMEO AND JULIET

Words by LARRY KUSIK and EDDIE SNYDER
Music by NINO ROTA

Copyright © 1968 (Renewed 1996) by Famous Music Corporation
International Copyright Secured   All Rights Reserved

TIME IN A BOTTLE

Words and Music by
JIM CROCE

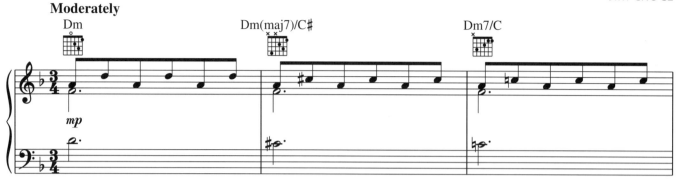

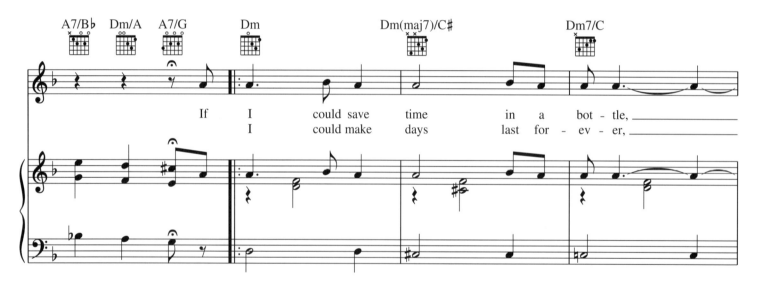

If I could save time in a bottle, _____
I could make days last for-ev-er, _____

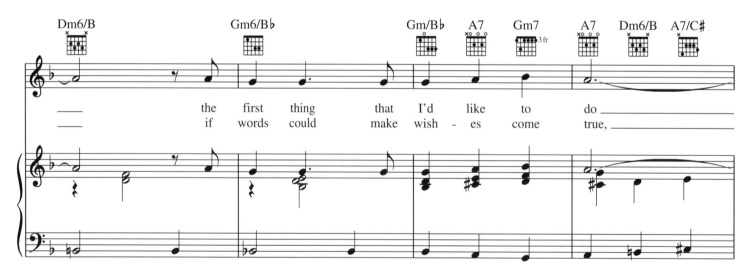

the first thing that I'd like to do _____
if words could make wish-es to come true, _____

Copyright © 1971 (Renewed) Time In A Bottle and Croce Publishing (ASCAP)
All Rights Reserved   Used by Permission

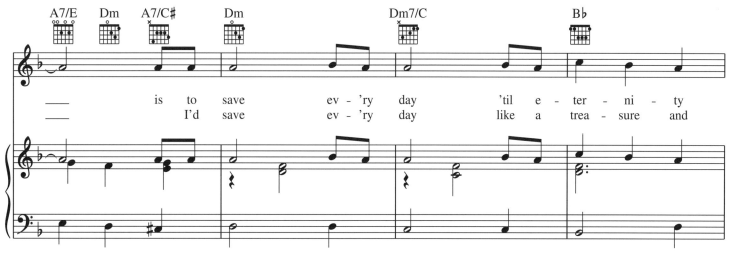

is to save ev - 'ry day 'til e - ter - ni - ty
I'd save ev - 'ry day like a trea - sure and

pass - es a - way just to spend them with you.
then a - gain I would spend them with you.

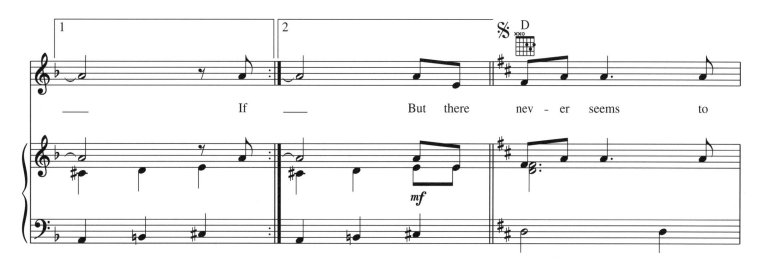

1

2

If But there nev - er seems to

be e - nough time to do the things you want to do once you

226

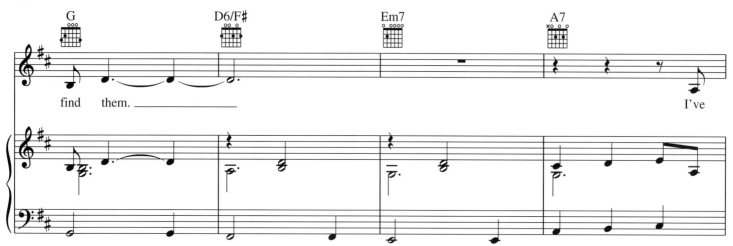

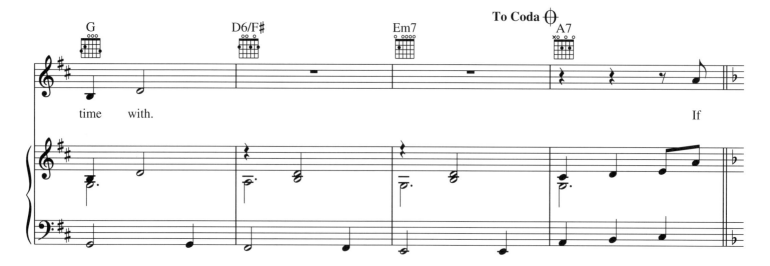

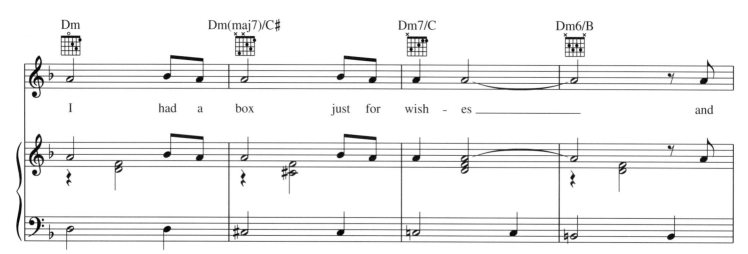

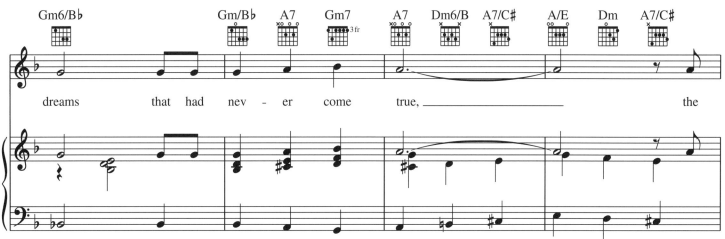

dreams that had nev - er come true, _____ the

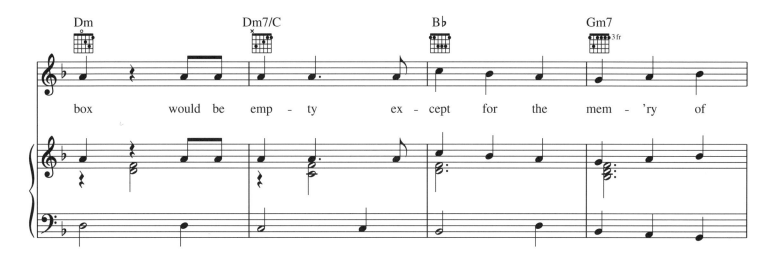

box would be emp - ty ex - cept for the mem - 'ry of

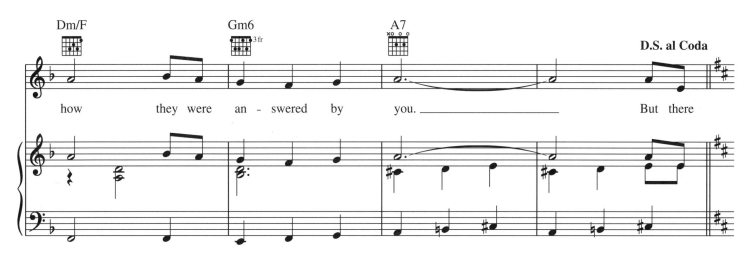

how they were an - swered by you. _____ But there

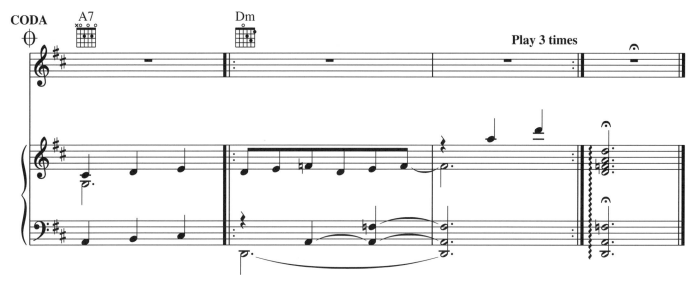

TOP OF THE WORLD

Words and Music by JOHN BETTIS
and RICHARD CARPENTER

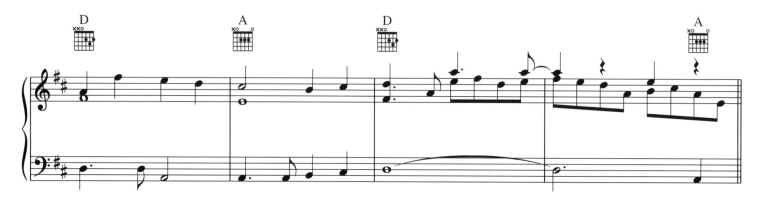

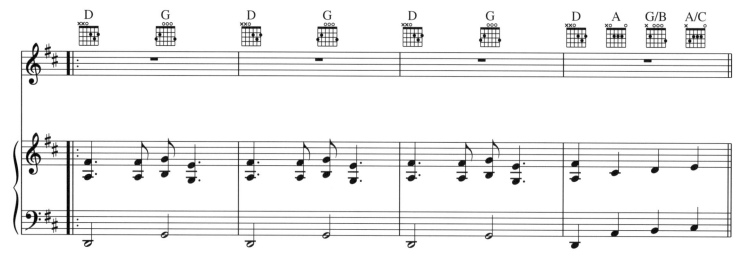

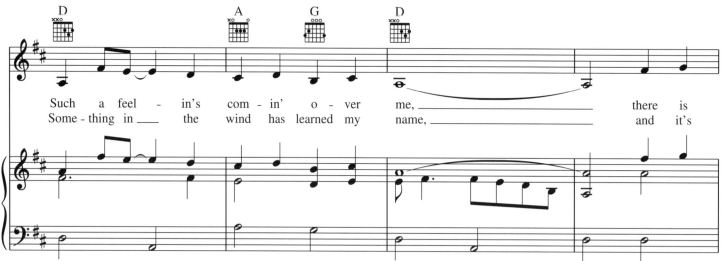

Such a feel - in's com - in' o - ver me, _____ there is
Some - thing in ___ the wind has learned my name, _____ and it's

Copyright © 1972 by ALMO MUSIC CORP. and HAMMER AND NAILS MUSIC
Copyright Renewed
All Rights Administered by ALMO MUSIC CORP.
All Rights Reserved   Used by Permission

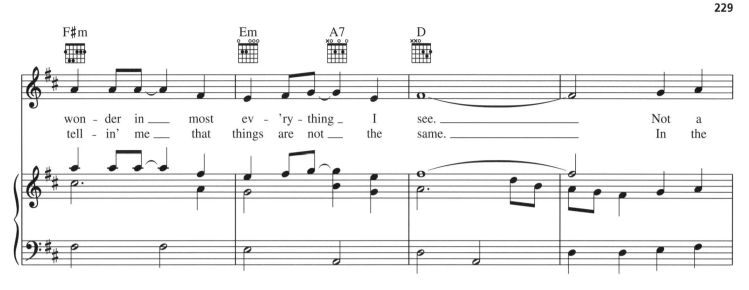

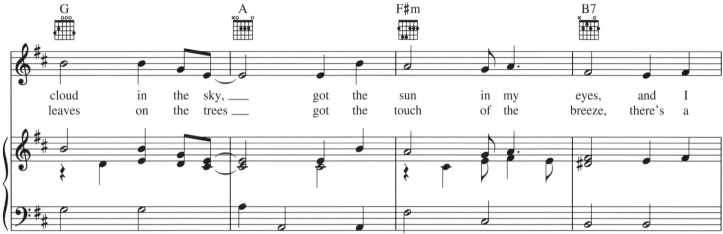

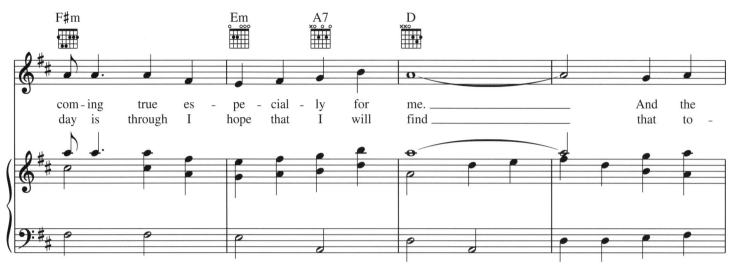

com-ing true es - pe - cial - ly for me. _____ And the
day is through I hope that I will find _____ that to -

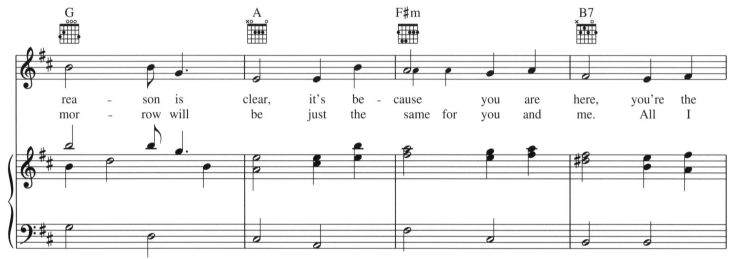

rea - son is clear, it's be - cause you are here, you're the
mor - row will be just the same for you and me. All I

near - est thing to heav - en that I've seen.
need will be mine if you are here.

I'm on the

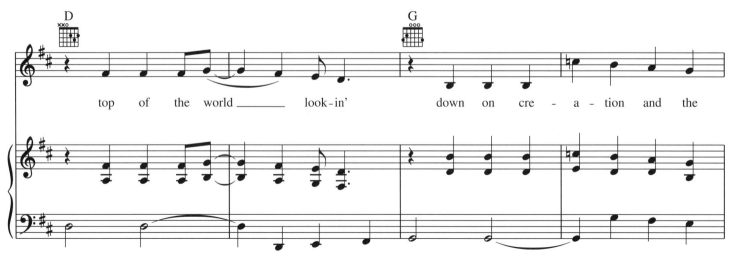

top of the world _____ look-in' down on cre - a - tion and the

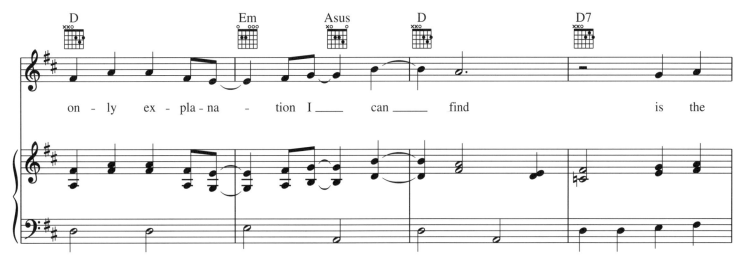

on - ly ex - pla - na - tion I ___ can ___ find is the

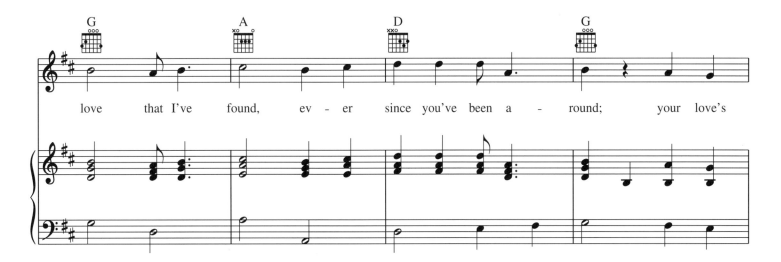

love that I've found, ev - er since you've been a - round; your love's

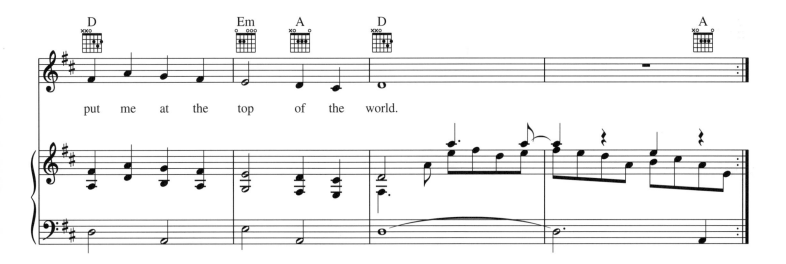

put me at the top of the world.

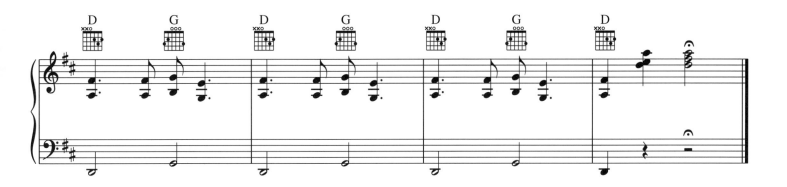

UNCHAINED MELODY

featured in the Motion Picture UNCHAINED

Lyric by HY ZARET
Music by ALEX NORTH

Moderately slow

Oh, my love, my dar - ling, I've hun - gered for your touch a long, lone - ly time. Time goes by so slow - ly and time can do so

© 1955 (Renewed) FRANK MUSIC CORP.
All Rights Reserved

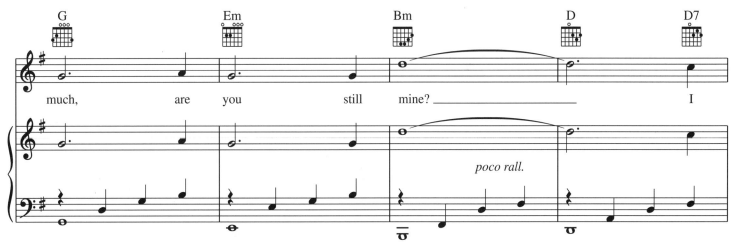

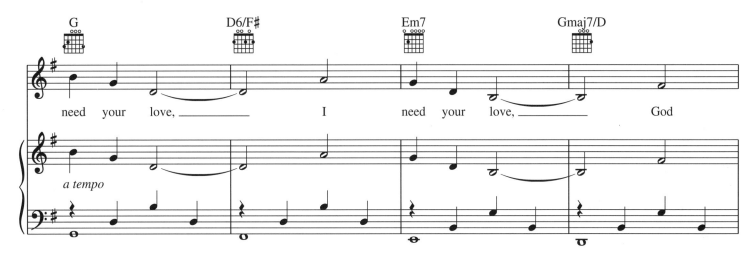

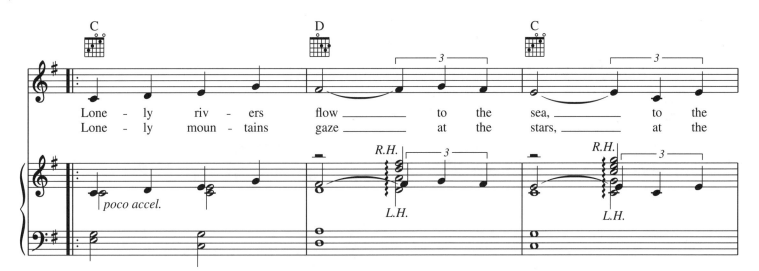

Tempo I

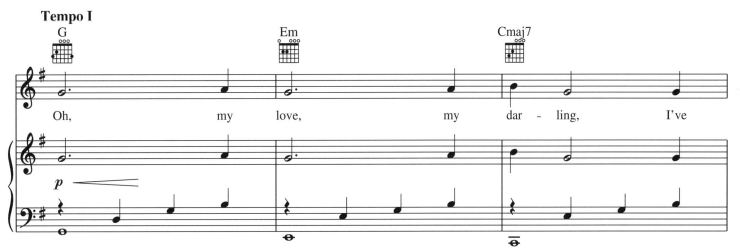

Oh, my love, my dar - ling, I've

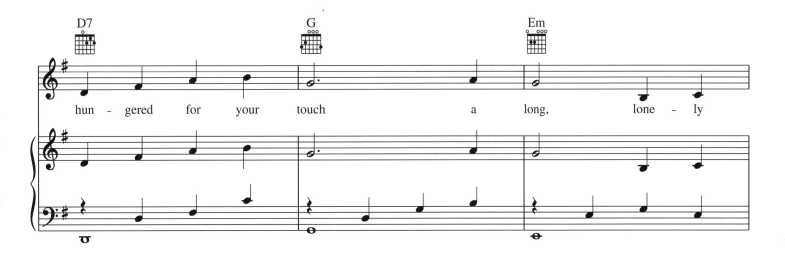

hun - gered for your touch a long, lone - ly

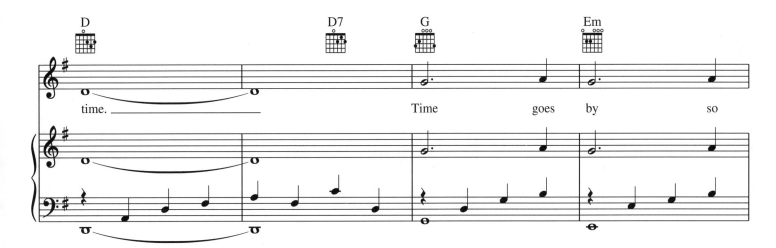

time. _____ Time goes by so

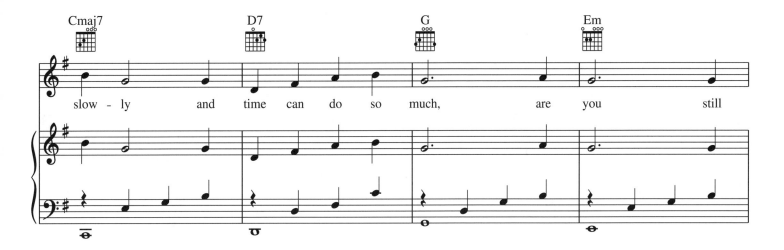

slow - ly and time can do so much, are you still

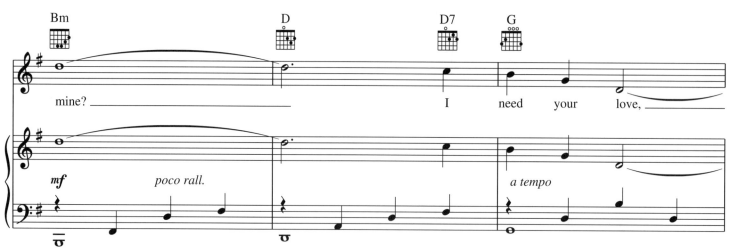

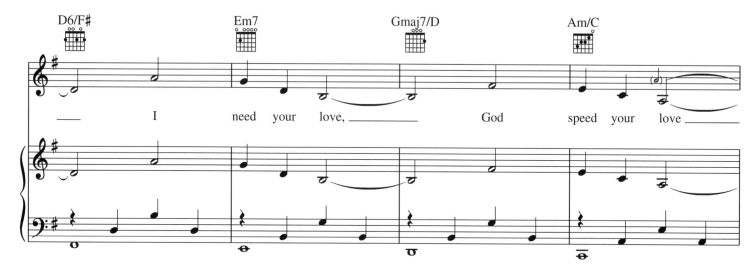

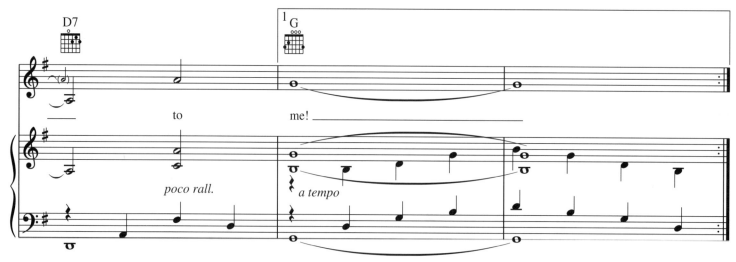

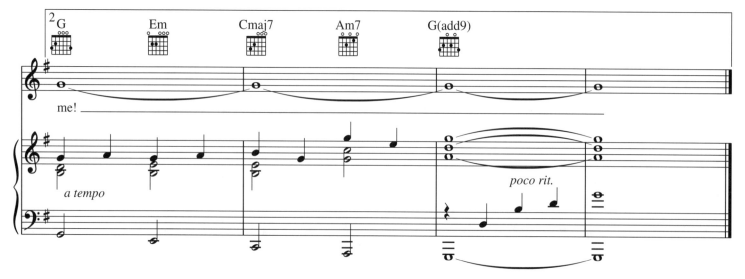

THE WAY WE WERE

Words by ALAN and MARILYN BERGMAN
Music by MARVIN HAMLISCH

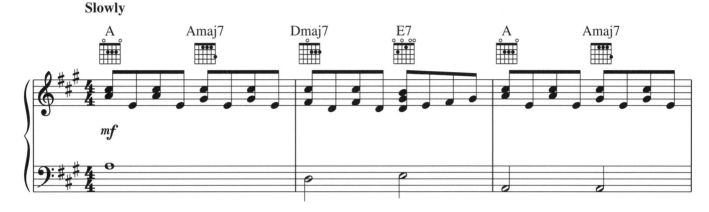

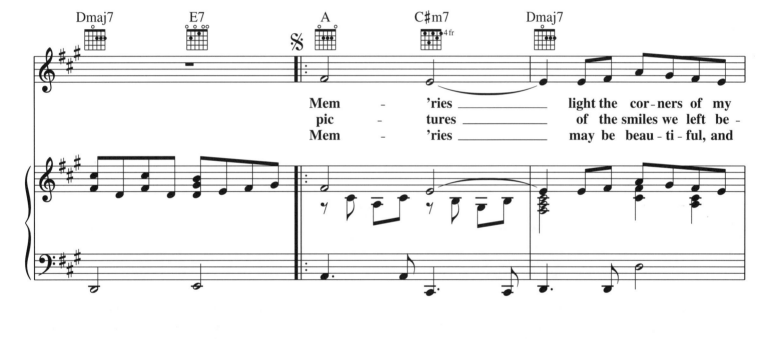

Mem - 'ries _____ light the cor-ners of my
pic - tures _____ of the smiles we left be -
Mem - 'ries _____ may be beau-ti-ful, and

mind.
hind,   Mist - y wa-ter-col-or mem - 'ries _____
yet,   smiles we gave to one an - oth - er _____
     what's too pain-ful to re - mem - ber

To Coda

© 1973 COLGEMS-EMI MUSIC INC.
All Rights Reserved   International Copyright Secured   Used by Permission

UNFORGETTABLE

Words and Music by
IRVING GORDON

Moderately

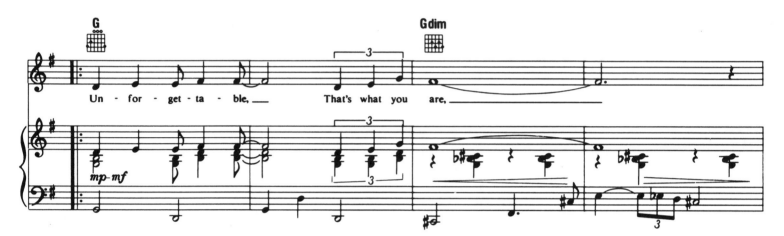

Un - for - get - ta - ble, ___ That's what you are, _____

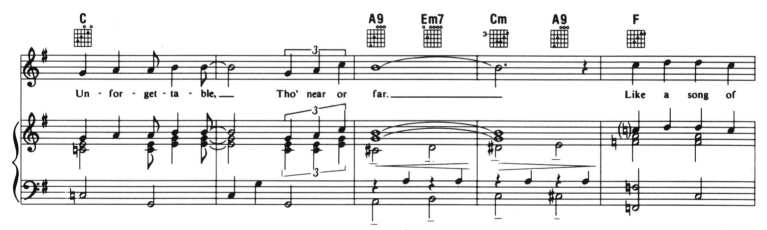

Un - for - get - ta - ble, ___ Tho' near or far. _____ Like a song of

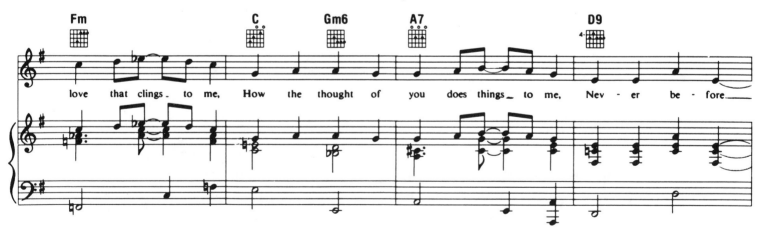

love that clings _ to me, How the thought of you does things _ to me, Nev - er be - fore ___

Copyright © 1951 by Bourne Co.
Copyright Renewed
International Copyright Secured   All Rights Reserved

WE'VE ONLY JUST BEGUN

Words and Music by ROGER NICHOLS
and PAUL WILLIAMS

Copyright © 1970 IRVING MUSIC, INC.
Copyright Renewed
All Rights Reserved   Used by Permission

244

WHEN YOU WISH UPON A STAR

Words by NED WASHINGTON
Music by LEIGH HARLINE

With expression

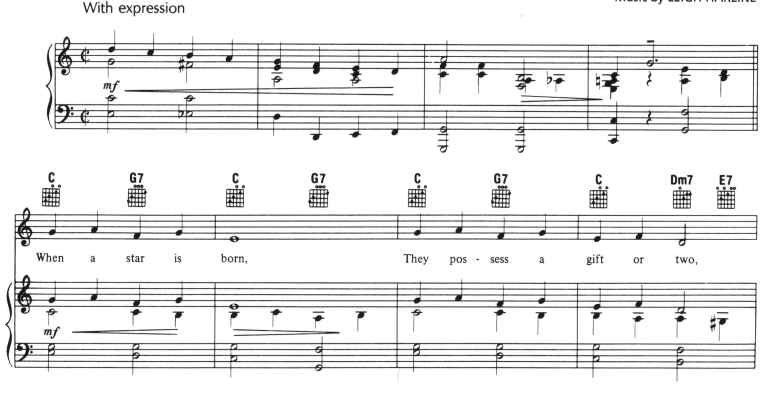

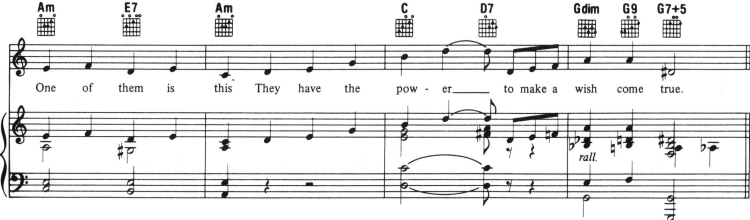

When a star is born, They pos-sess a gift or two,

One of them is this They have the pow-er____ to make a wish come true.

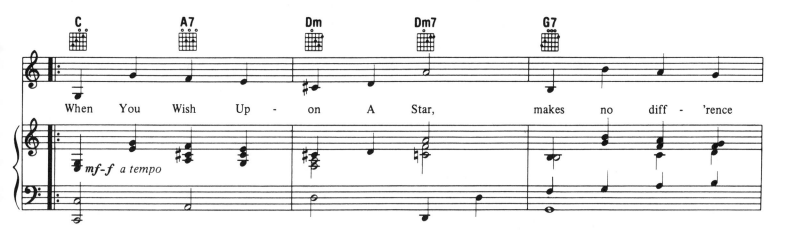

When You Wish Up - on A Star, makes no diff - 'rence

Copyright © 1940 by Bourne Co.
Copyright Renewed
International Copyright Secured   All Rights Reserved

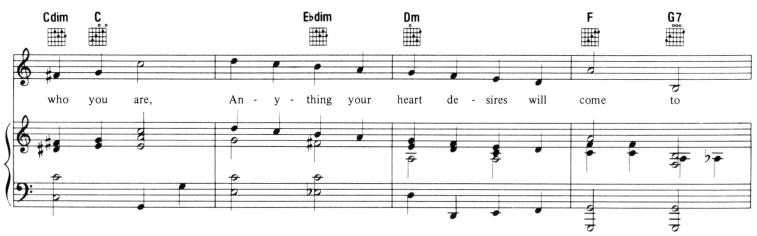

who you are, An - y - thing your heart de - sires will come to

you. If your heart is in your dream, no re - quest is

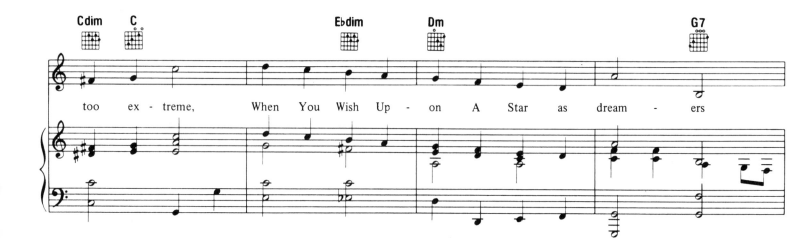

too ex - treme, When You Wish Up - on A Star as dream - ers

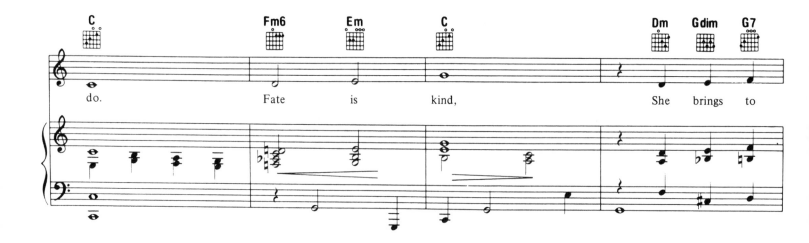

do. Fate is kind, She brings to

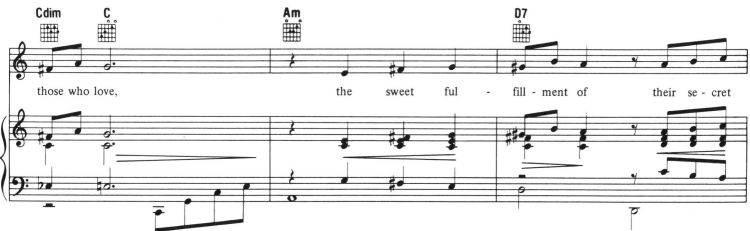

those who love, the sweet ful - fill - ment of their se - cret

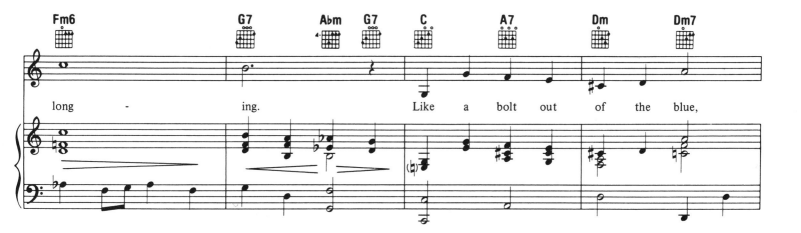

long - ing. Like a bolt out of the blue,

Fate steps in and sees you thru, When You Wish Up - on A Star your

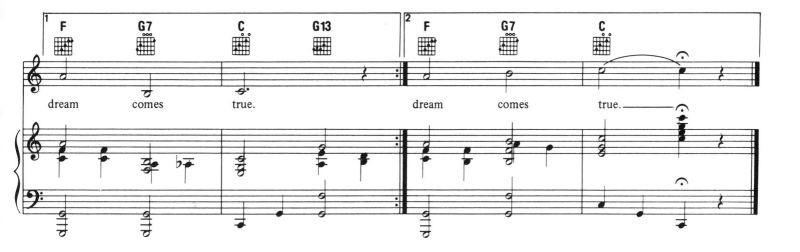

1. dream comes true.

2. dream comes true.

WHAT A WONDERFUL WORLD

Words and Music by GEORGE DAVID WEISS
and BOB THIELE

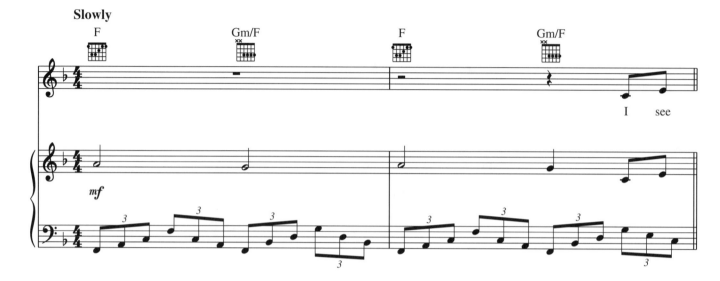

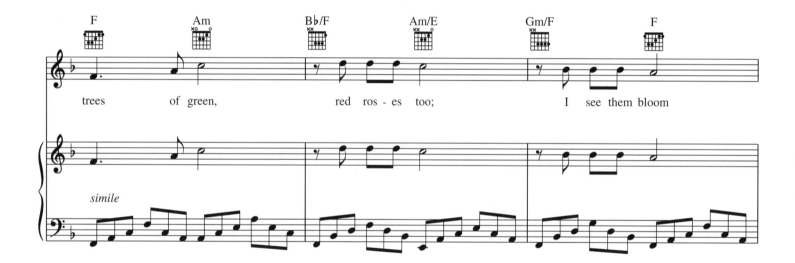

Copyright © 1967 by Range Road Music Inc., Quartet Music, Inc. and Abilene Music, Inc.
Copyright Renewed
International Copyright Secured   All Rights Reserved
Used by Permission

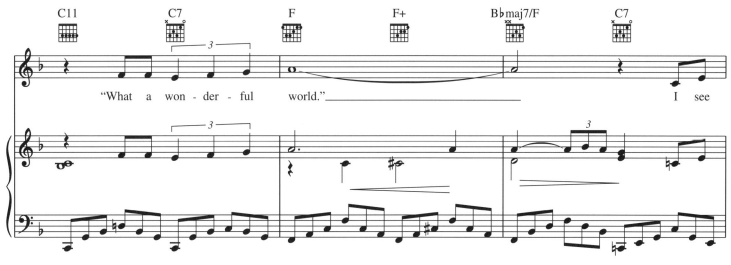

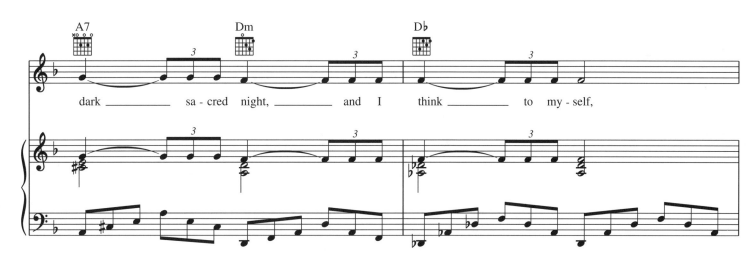

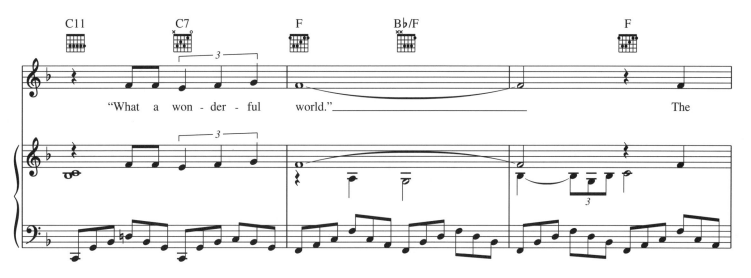

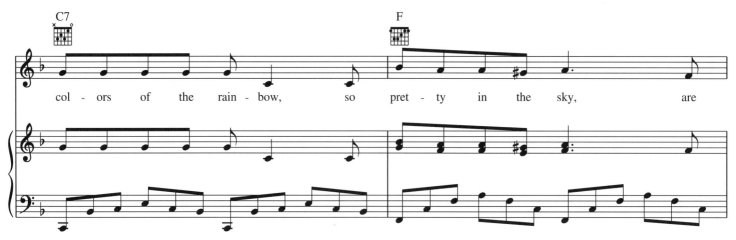

col - ors of the rain - bow, so pret - ty in the sky, are

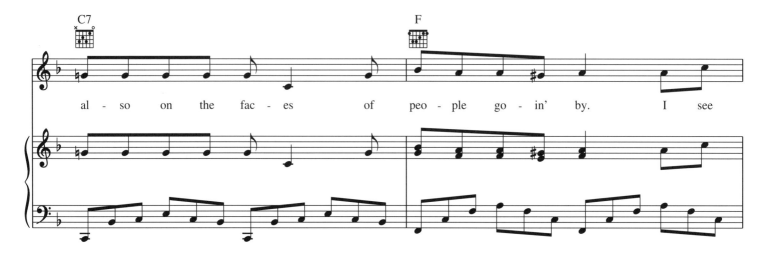

al - so on the fac - es of peo - ple go - in' by. I see

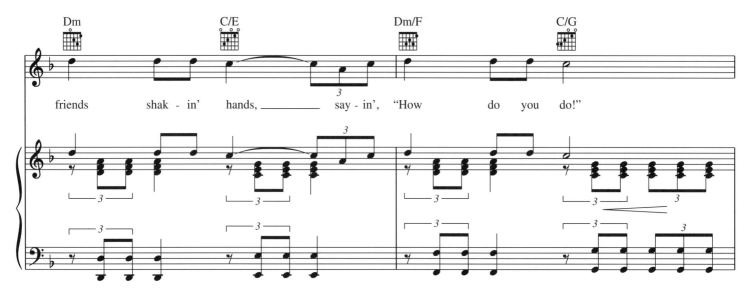

friends shak - in' hands, _____ say - in', "How do you do!"

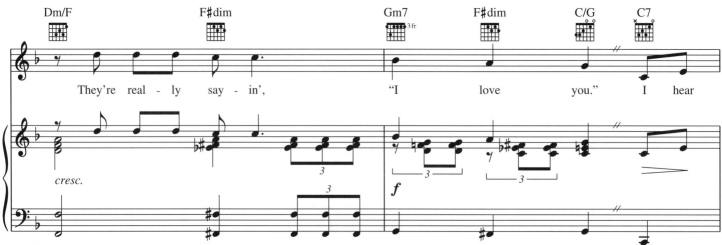

They're real - ly say - in', "I love you." I hear

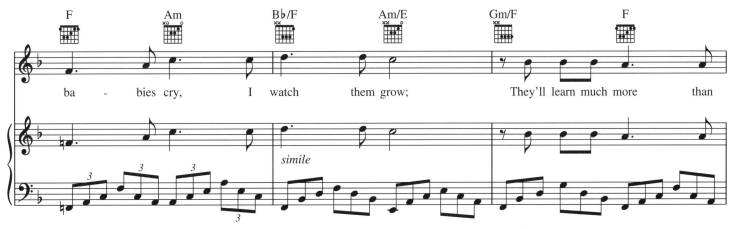

ba - bies cry, I watch them grow; They'll learn much more than

I'll _____ ev-er know, _____ and I think _____ to my-self, "What a won-der-ful

Rubato

world." _____ Yes, I think to my-self,

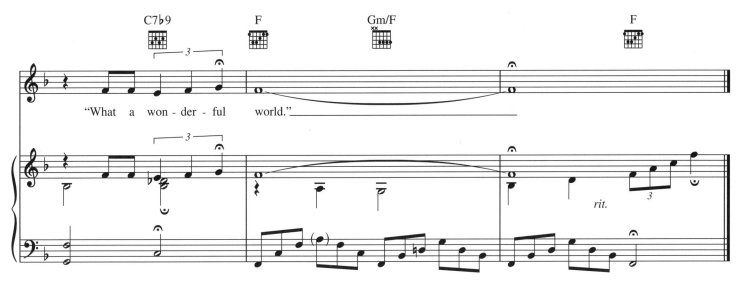

"What a won-der-ful world." _____

WHAT KIND OF FOOL AM I?

from the Musical Production STOP THE WORLD—I WANT TO GET OFF

Words and Music by LESLIE BRICUSSE
and ANTHONY NEWLEY

© Copyright 1961 (Renewed) TRO Essex Music Ltd., London, England
TRO - Ludlow Music, Inc., New York, controls all publication rights for the U.S.A. and Canada
International Copyright Secured
All Rights Reserved Including Public Performance For Profit
Used by Permission

WHEN I FALL IN LOVE

from ONE MINUTE TO ZERO

Words by EDWARD HEYMAN
Music by VICTOR YOUNG

Slowly, with much feeling

Copyright © 1952 by Chappell & Co. and Intersong U.S.A., Inc.
Copyright Renewed
International Copyright Secured   All Rights Reserved

WHERE DO I BEGIN
(Love Theme)
from the Paramount Picture LOVE STORY

Words by CARL SIGMAN
Music by FRANCIS LAI

Slowly

Where do I be-gin _____ to tell the sto-ry of how
With her first hel-lo _____ she gave a mean-ing to this

great a love can be, _____ the sweet love sto-ry that is
emp-ty world of mine. _____ There'd nev-er be an-oth-er

old-er than the sea, the sim-ple truth a-bout the
love, an-oth-er time; she came in-to my life and

Copyright © 1970, 1971 by Famous Music Corporation
Copyright Renewed 1998, 1999 and Assigned to Famous Music Corporation and Major Songs Company
All Rights for the world excluding the U.S.A. Controlled and Administered by Famous Music Corporation
International Copyright Secured   All Rights Reserved

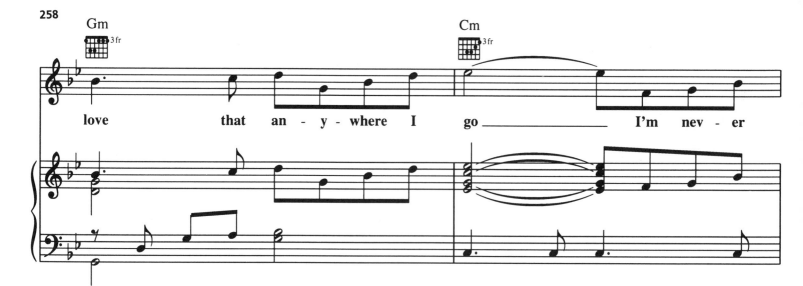

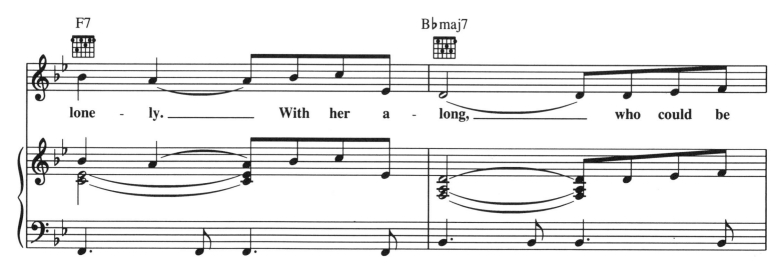

A WHOLE NEW WORLD
(Aladdin's Theme)
from Walt Disney's ALADDIN

Music by ALAN MENKEN
Lyrics by TIM RICE

© 1992 Wonderland Music Company, Inc. and Walt Disney Music Company
International Copyright Secured   All Rights Reserved

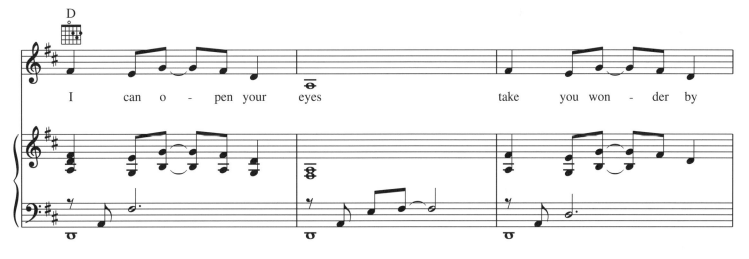

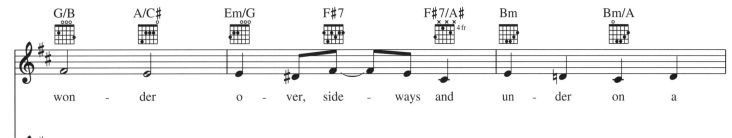

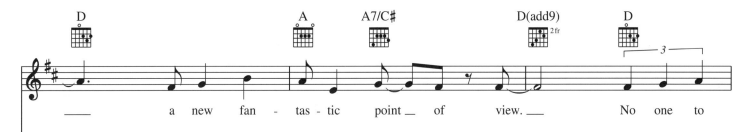

262

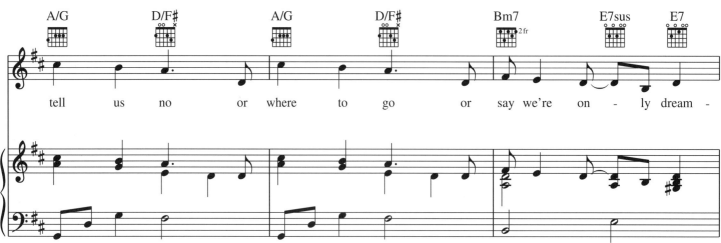

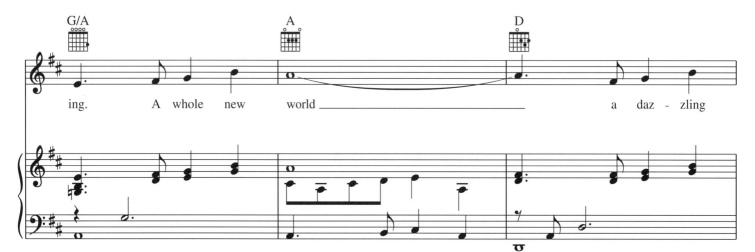

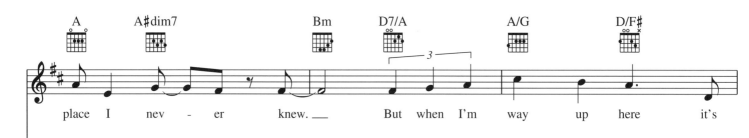

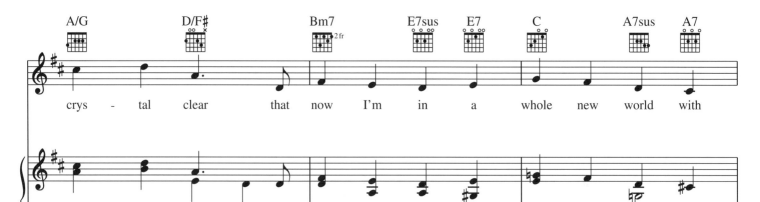

you. _____ Un - be - liev - a - ble

sights in - de - scrib - a - ble feel - ing.

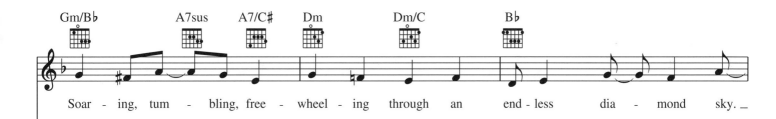

Soar - ing, tum - bling, free - wheel - ing through an end - less dia - mond sky. _

_ A whole new world _____ a hun - dred thou - sand things be -

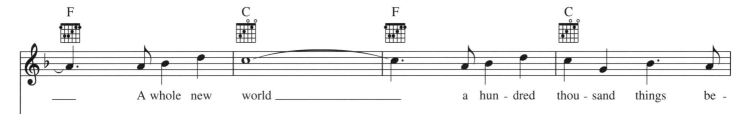

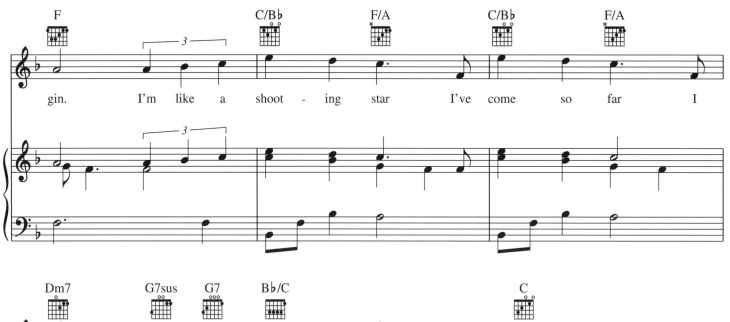

gin. I'm like a shoot - ing star I've come so far I

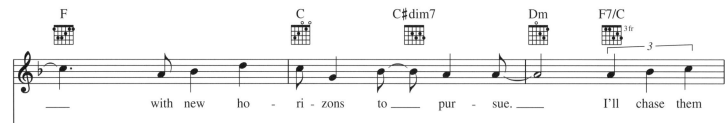

can't go back. I'm in a whole new world _____

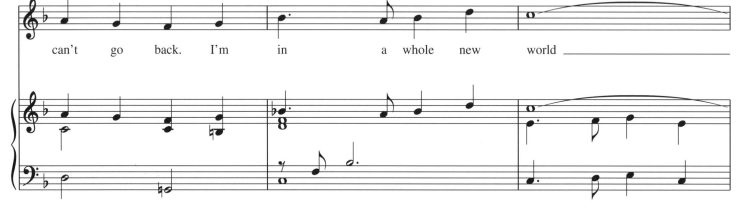

_____ with new ho - ri - zons to ___ pur - sue. ___ I'll chase them

an - y - where. There's time to spare. Let me share this

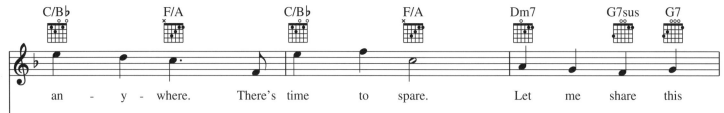

YESTERDAY

Words and Music by JOHN LENNON
and PAUL McCARTNEY

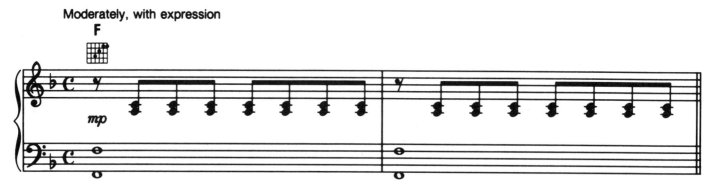

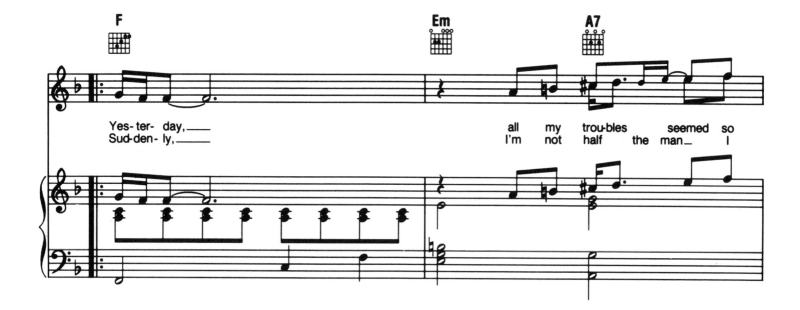

Yes-ter-day,___ all my trou-bles seemed so
Sud-den-ly,___ I'm not half the man_ I

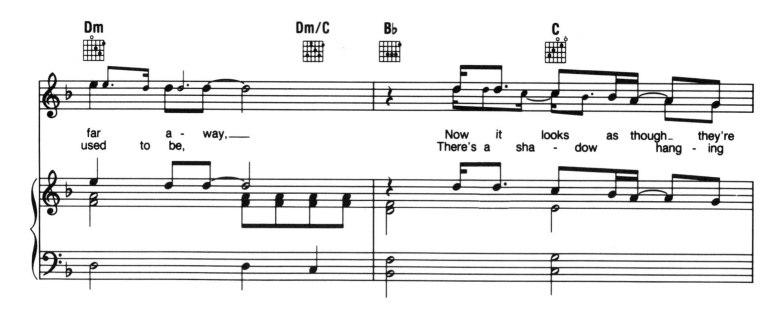

far a-way,___ Now it looks as though_ they're
used to be, There's a sha-dow hang-ing

Copyright © 1965 Sony/ATV Songs LLC
Copyright Renewed
All Rights Administered by Sony/ATV Music Publishing, 8 Music Square West, Nashville, TN 37203
International Copyright Secured All Rights Reserved

YOU ARE SO BEAUTIFUL

Words and Music by BILLY PRESTON
and BRUCE FISHER

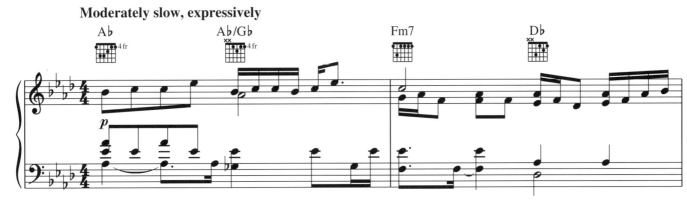

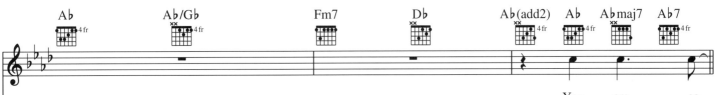

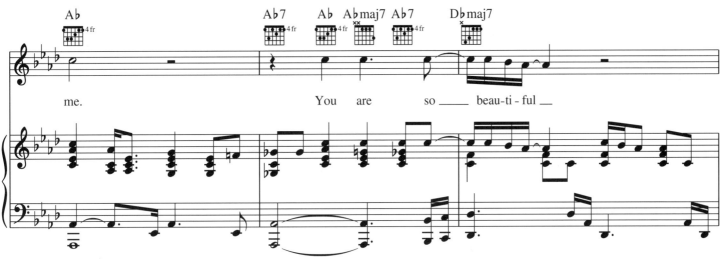

Copyright © 1973 IRVING MUSIC, INC. and ALMO MUSIC CORP.
Copyright Renewed
All Rights Reserved   Used by Permission

YOU ARE THE SUNSHINE
OF MY LIFE

Words and Music by
STEVIE WONDER

© 1972 (Renewed 2000) JOBETE MUSIC CO., INC. and BLACK BULL MUSIC
c/o EMI APRIL MUSIC INC.
All Rights Reserved   International Copyright Secured   Used by Permission

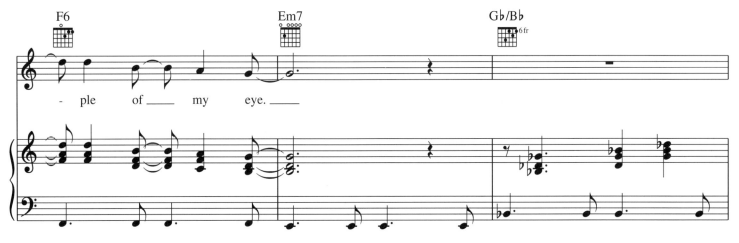

-ple of ___ my eye. ___

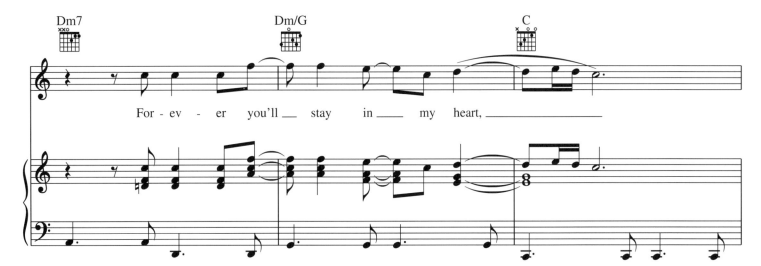

For - ev - er you'll ___ stay in ___ my heart, _____

I feel like this ___ is the ___ be -
You must have known ___ that I ___ was

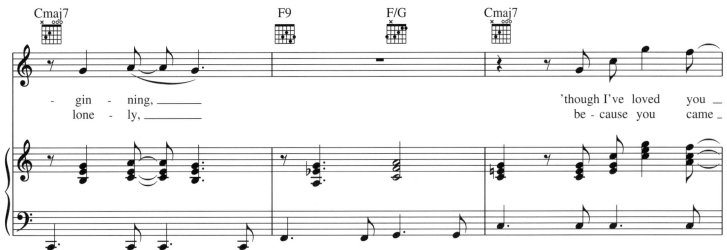

- gin - ning, _____
lone - ly, _____

'though I've loved you __
be - cause you came __

YOU'VE GOT A FRIEND

Words and Music by
CAROLE KING

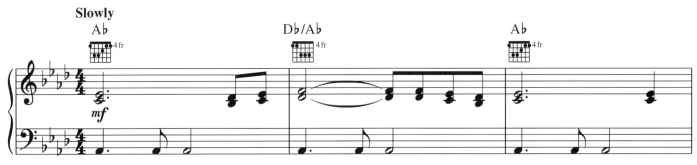

When you're down ___ and troub - led and you need ___
a - bove ___ you grows ___ dark ___

some love and care ___ and noth - in', ___
and full of clouds ___ and that ol' ___

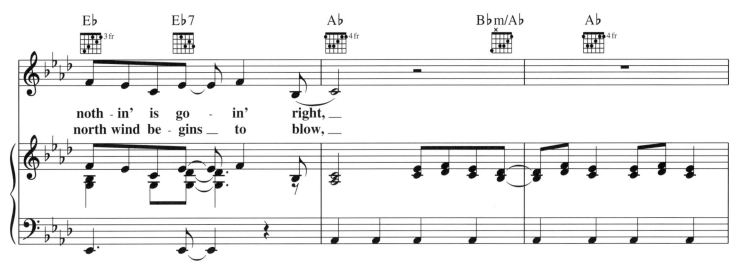

noth - in' is go - in' right, ___
north wind be - gins ___ to blow, ___

© 1971 (Renewed 1999) COLGEMS-EMI MUSIC INC.
All Rights Reserved   International Copyright Secured   Used by Permission

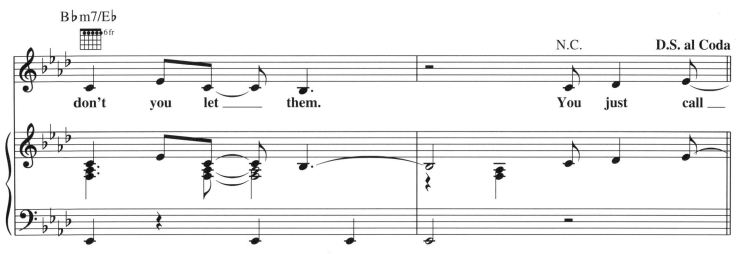

don't you let ____ them. You just call ___

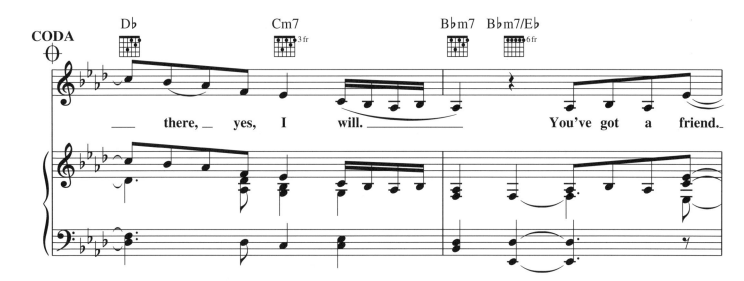

___ there, __ yes, I will. _____ You've got a friend._

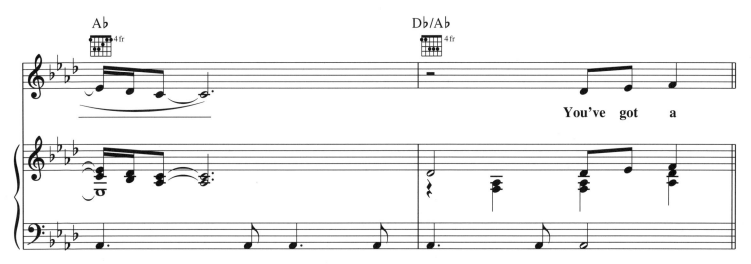

You've got a

friend. _____ Ain't it good ___ to know you've got a

The Greatest Songs Ever Written

THE BEST EVER COLLECTION
ARRANGED FOR PIANO, VOICE AND GUITAR

150 of the Most Beautiful Songs Ever
150 ballads: Edelweiss • For All We Know • How Deep Is Your Love • I'll Be Seeing You • Summertime • Unchained Melody • Young at Heart • many more.
00360735...$19.95

The Best Big Band Songs Ever
Over 60 big band hits: Boogie Woogie Bugle Boy • Don't Get Around Much Anymore • In the Mood • Moonglow • Sentimental Journey • Who's Sorry Now • more.
00359129...$16.95

The Best Broadway Songs Ever
Over 70 songs in all! Includes: All I Ask of You • Bess, You Is My Woman • Climb Ev'ry Mountain • Comedy Tonight • If I Were a Rich Man • Ol' Man River • more!
00309155...$20.95

The Best Christmas Songs Ever
More than 60 holiday favorites: Frosty the Snow Man • A Holly Jolly Christmas • I'll Be Home for Christmas • Rudolph, The Red-Nosed Reindeer • Silver Bells • more.
00359130...$18.95

The Best Classic Rock Songs Ever
Over 60 hits: American Woman • Bang a Gong • Cold As Ice • Heartache Tonight • Rock and Roll All Nite • Smoke on the Water • Wonderful Tonight • and more.
00310800...$17.95

The Best Classical Music Ever
Over 80 of classical favorites: Ave Maria • Canon in D • Eine Kleine Nachtmusik • Für Elise • Lacrymosa • Ode to Joy • William Tell Overture • and many more.
00310674...$17.95

The Best Contemporary Christian Songs Ever
Over 70 favorites, including: Awesome God • El Shaddai • Friends • Jesus Freak • People Need the Lord • Place in This World • Serve the Lord • Thy Word • more.
00310558...$19.95

The Best Country Songs Ever
78 classic country hits, featuring: Always on My Mind • Crazy • Daddy Sang Bass • Forever and Ever, Amen • God Bless the U.S.A. • I Fall to Pieces • Stand By Your Man • Through the Years • and more.
00359135...$17.95

The Best Early Rock N Roll Songs Ever
Over 70 songs, including: Book of Love • Crying • Do Wah Diddy Diddy • Louie, Louie • Peggy Sue • Shout • Splish Splash • Stand By Me • Tequila • and more.
00310816...$17.95

The Best Easy Listening Songs Ever
75 mellow favorites: (They Long to Be) Close to You • Every Breath You Take • How Am I Supposed to Live Without You • Unchained Melody • more.
00359193...$18.95

The Best Gospel Songs Ever
80 gospel songs: Amazing Grace • Daddy Sang Bass • How Great Thou Art • I'll Fly Away • Just a Closer Walk with Thee • Just a Little Talk with Jesus • The Old Rugged Cross • Will the Circle Be Unbroken • more.
00310503...$19.95

The Best Hymns Ever
118 of the most loved hymns of all time: Abide with Me • Every Time I Feel the Spirit • He Leadeth Me • I Love to Tell the Story • The Old Rugged Cross • Were You There? • When I Survey the Wondrous Cross • and more.
00310774...$17.95

The Best Jazz Standards Ever
77 jazz hits: April in Paris • Don't Get Around Much Anymore • Love Is Here to Stay • Misty • Satin Doll • Unforgettable • When I Fall in Love • and more.
00311641...$18.95

The Best Latin Songs Ever
67 songs, including: Besame Mucho (Kiss Me Much) • Blame It on the Bossa Nova • The Girl from Ipanema • Malaguena • One Note Samba • Slightly Out of Tune (Desafinado) • Summer Samba (So Nice) • and more.
00310355...$19.95

The Best Love Songs Ever
65 favorite love songs, including: Endless Love • Here and Now • Love Takes Time • Misty • My Funny Valentine • So in Love • You Needed Me • Your Song.
00359198...$17.95

The Best Movie Songs Ever
74 songs from the movies: Almost Paradise • Chariots of Fire • My Heart Will Go On • Take My Breath Away • Unchained Melody • You'll Be in My Heart • more.
00310063...$19.95

The Best R&B Songs Ever
66 songs, including: Baby Love • Endless Love • Here and Now • I Will Survive • Saving All My Love for You • Stand By Me • What's Going On • and more.
00310184...$19.95

The Best Rock Songs Ever
Over 60 songs: All Shook Up • Blue Suede Shoes • Born to Be Wild • Every Breath You Take • Free Bird • Hey Jude • We Got the Beat • Wild Thing • more!
00490424...$18.95

The Best Songs Ever
Over 70 must-own classics, including: All I Ask of You • Crazy • Edelweiss • Love Me Tender • Memory • My Funny Valentine • Tears in Heaven • Unforgettable • The Way We Were • A Whole New World • and more.
00359224...$22.95

More of the Best Songs Ever
79 more favorites: April in Paris • Candle in the Wind • Endless Love • Misty • My Blue Heaven • My Heart Will Go On • Stella by Starlight • Witchcraft • more.
00310437...$19.95

The Best Standards Ever, Vol. 1 (A-L)
72 beautiful ballads, including: All the Things You Are • Bewitched • Getting to Know You • God Bless' the Child • Hello, Young Lovers • It's Only a Paper Moon • I've Got You Under My Skin • The Lady Is a Tramp.
00359231...$15.95

The Best Standards Ever, Vol. 2 (M-Z)
72 songs, including: Makin' Whoopee • Misty • Moonlight in Vermont • My Funny Valentine • People Will Say We're in Love • Smoke Gets in Your Eyes • Strangers in the Night • Tuxedo Junction • Yesterday.
00359232...$15.95

More of the Best Standards Ever, Vol. 1 (A-L)
76 all-time favorites, including: Ain't Misbehavin' • Always • Autumn in New York • Body and Soul • Desafinado • Fever • Fly Me to the Moon • For All We Know • Georgia on My Mind • Lazy River • and more.
00310813...$17.95

More of the Best Standards Ever, Vol. 2 (M-Z)
75 more stunning standards: Makin' Whoopee! • Mona Lisa • Mood Indigo • Moon River • My Favorite Things • Norwegian Wood • Route 66 • Sentimental Journey • Stella by Starlight • What a Diff'rence a Day Made • What'll I Do? • You Are the Sunshine of My Life • more.
00310814...$17.95

FOR MORE INFORMATION, SEE YOUR LOCAL MUSIC DEALER, OR WRITE TO:

HAL•LEONARD™ CORPORATION
7777 W. BLUEMOUND RD. P.O. BOX 13819 MILWAUKEE, WI 53213

Visit us on-line for complete songlists.
www.halleonard.com

Prices, contents and availability subject to change without notice. Not all products available outside the U.S.A.